IN IRISH WATERWAYS

EDWARD O'REGAN

IN IRISH
WATERWAYS

CURRACH
PRESS

First published in 2005 by
CURRACH PRESS
55A Spruce Avenue, Stillorgan Industrial Park, Blackrock,
Co Dublin, Ireland

www.currach.ie

1 3 5 7 9 10 8 6 4 2

Cover design by Anú Design
Origination by Currach Press
Maps by Susan Waine
Printed by Betaprint Ltd, Dublin

ISBN 1-85607-915-5

Acknowledgements

The author and publisher gratefully acknowledge the assistance of
James O'Halloran SDB, Jenny Perkins FMA and Bríd O'Donohue in
bringing this book to fruition.

CONTENTS

	Preface	7
	Foreword	9
I	The Liffey	11
II	The Royal Canal and Midland Lakes	25
III	The Shannon and Lough Ree	59
IV	The Blackwater	85
V	The Brosna	109
VI	Lough Oughter	121
VII	The Corrib Lakes	137

PREFACE

To say that Ireland has changed rapidly and dramatically over the past few decades is a cliché. But it's also true, and this book demonstrates just how great the changes have been.

In Irish Waterways is about journeys made on the Irish inland waterways between 1939 and 1949 by Edward O'Regan. It was written some time later and then the typescript lay unpublished for many years. The result is a travel book that not only takes us on journeys along rivers, lakes and canals but also takes us on a journey back in time. We are visiting a foreign country – an Ireland that no longer exists.

Of course, the rivers, lakes and canals are still there and exploring them is still an adventure. In the 1980s I took my own tent and canoe on many of the same waterways that Edward O'Regan had paddled forty years previously. I didn't know about his explorations and I thought I was a pioneer.

I used a slightly different craft, an open Canadian style canoe made of fibreglass. I had abruptly terminated my relationship with kayaks some years previously after I borrowed one that was too small and got jammed in it going down a weir on the River Barrow upside down. I met many of the same problems as Edward O'Regan – bad weather, bullocks that trampled tents and wet provisions. But I also experienced the same sense of natural beauty, freedom and unexpected wilderness.

Nowadays a lot more people, Irish people and foreigners, are exploring our inland waters. Some of them are even using canoes to do so. They know the satisfaction of travelling by their own muscle power. They know the extra dimension that's revealed when you travel virtually soundlessly. They know the intimate relationship with nature that develops when you're low in the water in a frail craft. It's really quite different to looking at the river from the fly bridge of a twin screw diesel yacht.

When you start reading this book you react first of all to everything that has changed in this country in sixty years. But, if you love rivers and canals, you will end up being impressed by what is still the same. By the timeless and unchanging beauty of our waterscapes and how, even today, they can be channels leading to unspoiled wilderness.

Ireland is not as unhurried, not as friendly, not as safe as it once was. Many things have changed. Hunting badgers with a bow and arrow is not only illegal today, it's also unacceptable. Things were different then.

But the waterways still have the essential magic that is captured in this book. It will sit on that short section of my book shelves that's devoted to classic writing about the joys of inland boating.

Dick Warner
Gilltown
Co Kildare

August 2004

FOREWORD

This little book records some seven canoe trips made from 1939 up to about nine or ten years later.

Each trip lasted two weeks and we camped in a small tent on passage, except for the account on the Liffey, which was a weekend affair.

It was not intended to go into detail about famous or historical landmarks as guidebooks do this well enough. We were young and enthusiastic, and all we wanted was to discover those marvellous inland waters which a bountiful nature has lavished on this beautiful island, and to revel in that pursuit that Kenneth Grahame in *The Wind in the Willows* so aptly described: 'Believe me, my young friend, there is nothing – absolutely nothing – half so much worth doing as simply messing about in boats.'

What we didn't realise for many years later was our extraordinary luck in the particular time. Great numbers had left to join the British Army or to work in the war factories. There was practically no home industry, no motor cars, no petrol, and we had an almost deserted countryside to explore, completely crime-free, and everyone you met utterly trustworthy. Also, we were pioneers in such exploratory journeys, and indeed the canoe was as much a source of wonder to many, as to ourselves, on these wonderful trips.

There has been an enormous growth in the sport of canoeing since those times, but it has been almost exclusively of the fibre-class Slalom type, for white-water work. Recently, over one thousand canoes were said to have taken part in the Liffey Descent. I think, therefore, these inland voyages still remain unique, and indeed, at this stage, are a tiny historical frozen cameo, so much has Ireland and the world changed since then.

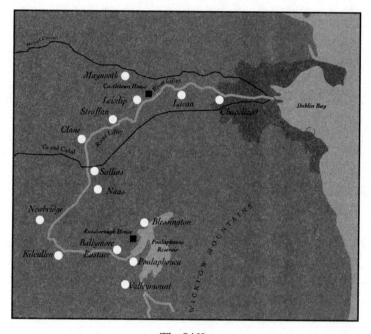

The Liffey

THE LIFFEY

It was upon one fine sunny day, sitting by the banks of the Liffey and dreaming under half-closed eyelids of the romance of rivers, that it came upon me how I had so carelessly neglected exploring them. I there and then decided to do something about it, for I was young and eager, and it seemed to me a good way of using up the superfluous energy of youth.

I talked over the idea with a sympathetic friend and after discussing the various modes of travel open to us, and having regard to that final arbiter of all desires, the purse, we chose. canoeing. For ease of transport, a collapsible. We knew little enough between us of canoeing, and nothing of collapsibles, but that was a small thing. So we saved up our shillings for many months, until one Saturday afternoon, I staggered out of a sports store with two great bags on my back, and walked with them to our wrestling club, near the River Liffey. It was a wonderful moment.

Nevertheless, that evening when we spilled the contents of the bags onto the floor, we were appalled at the incredible heap of junk that confronted us. Sitting down with our explanation leaflet, written in German, of which neither of us understood a word, and following the diagrams, after hours of foostering with stays, ferrules, ribs, bolts, butterfly nuts and canvas, we, in the early hours of the morning, unearthed the 'Hart' De Luxe Sports collapsible canoe. She was very handsome. These were her dimensions:

| Weight 55 lbs | Load capacity 500 lbs | Length 18 feet |
| Breadth 3 feet | Depth 1½ feet | Draft 4½ inches |

There are not many waterways in Ireland that cannot be navigated in a craft with a four-and-a-half inch draft.

Early on the following Sunday morning we tried her out on the Liffey. We wanted no inquisitive idlers poking barbs of wit at us on our first trip and the city was deserted when, without the champagne and the cheers, we timorously commenced our maiden voyage. We called her *Minny*.

At first I thought her wonderfully unsafe. She was very lightly loaded and rocked if you sneezed. It did not seem likely we would travel a mile without a spill. No doubt this is a common experience with beginners. There was a great clashing of paddles, much splashing, a little nervous cursing and a prodigious going around in circles. After progressing from circling to zig-zagging, we came to the first weir. *Minny* was light as a feather to carry and in the summer months weirs usually have a dry spot suitable for portages. In a matter of minutes we had her floating on the upper reach of the river.

An outraged swan gave chase as we passed the weir, giving us an anxious ten minutes, but we made a great bluster with our paddles and roared loudly, so that he respected us as veterans and let us pass. The actor in us is easily brought out and Benny and I put on a show for each other's benefit and encouragement.

Gradually we learned to synchronise the eight-feet long double paddles, making a fair pace. The city environs dropped behind, leaving us alone on the smooth and quiet rural stretches, passing among tall trees with a quiet motion. Perhaps it is this unique peacefulness that is the peculiar charm of canoeing. In no other craft do you get such soundless motion, such ease and fluency of travel. As there are no rowlocks, the only sound is the splash of the paddles and with a little experience, even this becomes almost inaudible as the long slow sweep of long distance travelling is acquired. It is quite a dreamy sort of journeying, conducive to soliloquy. Much talking is not encouraged, for one is jealous of distractions, and as restfulness settles over the busy mind and lulls it to reflection, then, as if by tacit consent, speech is shortened to monosyllables.

Now and again, as it was high summer, and the river consequently very low, we had to take to wading. This is a little more difficult than it seems, and can be recommended for hardening tender feet. It is wise to bring a pair of old shoes specially for this purpose; and the older the shoes the better, for they receive a rough time. We both wore bathing trunks, for it was warm and sunny and an excellent opportunity to acquire a tan.

My shipmate led the way, the long fore-painter stretched taut over his brawny shoulders as he towed the canoe against the stream. I stumbled along guiding her from the stern.

It was an ease to paddle in the cool water as long as you watched where you were going. Once Benny did not, as he was heaving away in fairly deep water among rocks. Here we towed, owing to the strong current, not because of shallows. My friend suddenly disappeared from view with a splash and a series of gurgles. *Minny* slewed around and started back at a gathering speed. I dived rapidly after her, catching the floating painter in time to heave her off a half-sunken tree. It taught us to keep our eyes open. You can never be too careful when wading in unknown waters.

We pitched camp at evening about a mile below Lucan. The river here had wandered away from the road, and flowed silently and deeply between a tall aisle of giant beeches and sycamores. The right bank rose precipitously behind them and we made our night-rest in a little clearing below the highland. Occasionally a loud splash in the gathering dusk told of a salmon rise and once, we saw a large fish lazing in the shallows in the last rays of the sun. His dorsal fin showed above the water as he lay motionless on the sand, dozing. The background of birdsong gradually faded as we took the canoe up on high ground for the night. The twilight mist arose spectrally from the waters, cooling the heat of the day and when the full moon shone through the trees it became chilly. We donned our pullovers and leather jackets and built up the fire with large logs.

It is, without doubt, a fine thing to lie down at night to sleep near a river. The thin fabric of the tent glows with a faint luminosity in the light of the moon. Outside is heard the little gurgles of the river, as if talking to itself, the splash of a rise, the distant bark of an otter. In the faint distance the weird call of a curlew echoes like the cry of a lost soul. Quiet and secret thoughts nestle close to the mind, *sympathica* with the night. Sleep comes late, often not late enough. I was in the nebulous land of the half-awake, drowsing on the events of the day and the dim speculations of the morrow.

Up with the sun, we walked over the dew-drenched fields to Mass in Lucan. From the high viaduct that spans the Liffey we sized up our chances of crossing the weir. The Lucan weir is one of the biggest on the whole river and, for a canoeist, very difficult of approach. For hundreds of yards the shallow river is studded with rocks and boulders and there is quite a strong flow. Even if one should succeed in bringing up safely to the weir-foot, the going gets worse upriver. At Leixlip, for instance, there was a miniature Grand Canyon where the narrowed river was measled with rocks and swept through them at a powerful rate. This stretch is now contained in the hydro-electric scheme.

We decided to stay below Lucan. As we had the whole day, before us, and such a comparatively short stretch of river to fool about on, we lazed around our camping spot all afternoon. The diversions to be had about a camp are many, limited only by the curiosity and ingenuity of the camper. For instance, after breakfast, if one is lucky enough to have a blazing sun, there is the pastime of plunging into a stretch of rapidly flowing water and streaking downstream at a breakneck speed. This is to be recommended only to those who keep their eyes above water-level when doing the crawl. Alternatively, if you are of the energetic type, you can turn around and thrash madly upstream. This usually gives a nice steady downstream drift, and you can get home after the style of the Irish schoolboy going to school, but will be much more exhausted.

Again, take the innumerable and endless chores of the camp; hewing or gathering timber, cleaning pots (they should be cleaned at least every two days!), mending torn clothes, tidying up after the indescribable confusion that periodically breaks out in every tent. This latter phenomenon will be well known to campers. In the morning, upon rising, the blankets are reasonably neat, the paraphernalia of eatables and perishables are still stacked tidily where they were laid the night before. Then you get up to cook breakfast. You remember you wish to find your spot on the map and you turn out the kit-bag. What's this? O yes, your anthology. Now what could be better than to start the morning with a few verses of Omar? You commence to read, pulling the blankets over your knees to keep out that sharp morning wind. Your confrère then asks you to hand him his shaving-soap and the search begins. When the contents of all the bags are thoroughly peppered amongst the blankets, the shaving-soap is discovered in the billy-can. From then on, chaos takes over. You take your foot out of the butter and look resignedly at the pool of tinned milk slowly and stickily soaking into your shirt. One develops fortitude after a few sessions and gives up the vain attempt to keep a well-ordered house.

However, if you have nothing else to do, the laudable, if Sisyphus-like toil, may be attempted, for nothing looks better than a neat, tidy, well-ordered tent interior. Twice, I think, I beheld this rarest of sights, and spent a while rhapsodizing on it, but few believed me. We usually dropped the tent-flaps when strangers approached and sidled quickly outside to avoid their inquisitive peering.

Then, of course, you can try some fishing or hunting, if you have a gun. Or even guggling trout, which is a fascinating way of wasting time. Guggling involve putting one's hand under a resting trout and waggling the fingers before lifting them out. The waggling must mesmerise the fish for a few seconds. The first time I tried it I actually had the fish in the palm of my hand, after ages of manoeuvring and careful positioning. Somehow he got away, but then I think my mentor had inadvertently omitted a lesson.

I once spoke to a man whose brother had known an old recluse living in the hills who had, he said, caught all his fish by this adroit technique. Outside of a magazine photograph of a countryman engaged in this occult science, I never came nearer than this to a first-hand experience of it. But they tell me it can be done quite easily – if you have the patience.

One thing is certain, you need never be idle around a tent, and he will be a busy man who has both a tent and a boat to look after. But there is one essential thing you must have, if you are to be happy messing about with a boat. You must have music. A boat without music never sailed, or, if it did, it must indeed have been a dull affair. All sailing ships had music. Why, even the old Black-Ball Liners creaked their capstans, heaved their anchors and hauled their massive sheets to rousing full-blooded shanties. How else have 'Billy Boy', 'Shenandoah', 'The Bay of Biscay' and scores of others come down to us but by the spirit of living welling up in a man as he battles with the cruel sea? Cold rationalists will say that shanties are a mere convenience, a metronome to measure equal strain; they know nothing of the fountains of the heart – else would not mere counting do?

I am not quite sure that there has been such a loyalty shown to the muse in the inland waters, but it is reasonable to assume that some of these boatmen must have maintained the great tradition. At any rate it is an indisputable fact that, once in a boat, this atavistic urge rises in one like a tide, and even shy men, who would not sing on dry land to save their lives, break into a gentle self-conscious murmuring when they feel the mystic exhilaration of a rocking boat.

To keep this fine tradition we felt was an obligation. So, as we dallied home, we roared out unisons and duets that frightened the timid water fowl from their feeding. We felt the better of it and the devil himself could not have shut us up. As an added homage Benny had brought along his guitar, and when we had exhausted the first animal feelings by bellowing shanties, he trolled more lyrical strains to its accompaniment. There being neither need nor urge to toil at pace-making, we made holiday and drifted at a snail's pace with the sluggish current, stretched out fully on the frail bottom, and keeping way and direction with a leisurely and occasional sweep of a paddle. As an interlude a verse would be recited, or perhaps a noble declamation out of a play; but this was by the way and depended on the scenery. It would be a sacrilege in certain lovely stretches to have to listen to 'The Wreck of the Bugaboo' or 'Slatterys Mounted Fut'. These were kept for the more banal parts, as also such inconsequences as 'Old King Cole'.

The canoe was vowed a success. Indeed we considered we had found our sea-legs, or perhaps I should say our river-bottoms, for one cannot stand up in a canoe. At least it is not to be recommended, especially when she is under way in deep water. There is, I believe, a very rigid rule for small-boat sailors, 'Never, never, belay the mainsheet.' And the basic axiom for canoeists is 'Never, never, stand up in a canoe.' One enters in a kind of crouch, making sure to hold both gunwales to maintain stability and sits down instantly. Similarly, on getting out, one member holds the canoe steady against the river bank, and the departee, first putting one foot ashore, holds a gunwale and the bank in either hand, and stands up quickly; or if it should be a high bank, eases himself gently onto it and worms upwards. Only once in a number of years did I see our little boat capsize, and that was with two great awkward fellows who insisted on standing up in fast-running water. They got the ducking they deserved, but they lost me a paddle.

Many times afterwards we 'did' the Liffey and found it to be a fine solacing kind of river. Those Dubliners, city of the city, who know her only as a glaucous stream that stinks in summer and rears a bitter wind in winter, would marvel at the 'sylvan beauty of the Liffey Vale', to use an advertising slogan popular on the now extinct tram. And this sylvan beauty does exist, as anyone who has boated from Islandbridge onwards will tell you. But the journey must be done all the way by river to fully appreciate it and the Tramway Co took a lot on themselves when they advised seeing it from their lumbering top-decks. This way one could get but glimpses of the river and its copses, whereas the true delight is to drift amongst its meadows and by old-world gardens, by the willow-clustered bends and the cuttings guarded by tall sentinel beeches and chestnuts that have stood in age-long patience whispering over Anna Liffey as she slowly makes her way to the City of the Dark Pool. The term 'Anna' is not an endearment but a corruption of the Irish word *amhain* for river.

Speaking of dark pools I have one unpleasant recollection of Anna that taught me to have a little more respect for her variable moods. This time there were three of us and every time there were three messing around *Minny*, something went wrong. Of course three did not travel in her, but two of us set out in the late evening to meet a third friend at an agreed weir, well upriver. Number three had waited patiently for hours, standing like a sentry on the watchtower, scanning the lower river from his vantage on the weir-head. In between the lonesome vigils he solaced himself with copious draughts at the hostelry conveniently situated but a hundred yards away. By the time we arrived, though discouraged by his long wait, he was tolerably well fortified against further disappointments. Having made a quick meal on the far bank, I, from old training, and despite repeated pleas to leave the work until after a 'refresher', pitched camp. It is a sound old maxim, 'First take care of the horse; then the man.'

The river, I noticed, as we walked over the dry lip of the weir, was very low, a mere trickle of water dribbling over one corner. Against my better judgment and instinct I forbore to cross in the canoe, and we tied her near the tent.

The pub was dark, lit by a single gloomy oil-lamp, and was crowded with men from local parts, farmers, labourers and mechanics who could have been met with in any country pub. The sprawling suburbs of the city had not yet engulfed them, but their days were numbered. It was an anachronism, this little public house within four miles of Dublin. It had a large bay latticed window, a very low and smoke-begrimed ceiling, an uneven flagged floor and a long unpolished counter, washed pale from the spilling of innumerable pints. It was clearly of another age.

Here we drank until midnight. One of our number, on the adjurations of a persistent peasant, trolled a rebel song and thereby damned himself, for they called for encores until he sang himself hoarse, then launched into animated discussion with a group of other rebels and ended up at midnight having lost all sense of time and location. Indeed the three of us were drunk on conviviality and bad beer.

When finally we were ushered onto the unfriendly road, all was dark and silent. There was no moon, no stars, no street-lights, and the few cottages around were in complete darkness. But we cared little and staggered off into the inky night, arm-in-arm, still, God forgive us, singing rebel songs, to escort one member a little of the way home, for he had far to go and was not staying in the camp.

An hour or so later, now a little sobered by the cool night air, we two walked back to our weir. We used two boxes of matches merely to find our way to the river through brambles, nettles, streams and potholes. And then, thoroughly sobered, we discovered that the weir was in full spate, roaring merrily over the whole wide lip. We tried to cross, but in the pitch blackness it was impossible. After meditation, I remembered an old private bridge that crossed the river some miles downriver. Thither we walked and with trouble scaled a ten-foot wall, only to find that the gates leading to the bridge were locked. And so we wearily lay down under a pine tree, judging we could sleep on the soft needles until light came. The effort lasted fifteen minutes exactly. The cold dews quickly soaked through our light clothes and our teeth chattered.

It struck me that benighted travellers of whom I had read, who settled comfortably under the starry sky to doze the summer nights away, had not lived in Ireland with its chill damp nights. And though in Spenser's time the Irish were wont to sleep under the open sky, wrapped in their mantles, as he has it: 'When it raineth it is his pent-house; when it bloweth, it is his tent; when it freezeth, it is his tabernacle.' Still, we are not of the iron that these hardy ancestors seem to have been made, and even with this wonderful mantle, which for its manifold uses (and abuses) Spenser would have had abolished altogether, I doubt if our modern Irishman could sleep for thirty minutes in the open at night.

Worn out with walking and yearning for sleep we came to the ubiquitous weir again, now in the first grey light at dawn. It was apparent that the locks above at Lucan had been opened during the night and there was no point in waiting for the weir flow to subside. As a last resort I had to strip and plunge into the cold river above the weir, and taking the canoe across, I ferried my comrade over to the welcome blankets of the tent, where, at 6 a.m. we turned in and slept the sleep of babes until noon.

Since then I have remembered that rivers may suddenly rise in the night, and a lesson thus bought at the cost of a night's sleep, is not quickly forgotten.

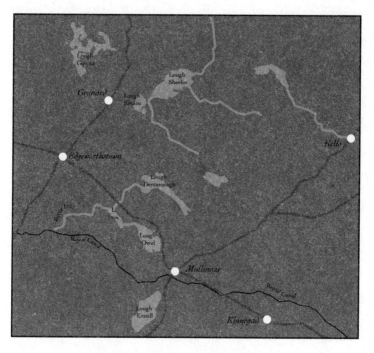

Royal Canal and Midland Lakes

THE ROYAL CANAL AND MIDLAND LAKES

We had a deal of trouble and wrangling in the choosing of our first itinerary. I was all for a short quiet little river, not too deep and with convenient banks. Not so my bold Benny. His experience was, by any standard, limited. But it was greater than mine, for I had never been out on a lake in a boat of any description, much less in a canoe. And though I was becoming canoe-conscious, I was ignorant of their capacities on open water. But Ulysses had been out on the Lower Lake at Glendalough (which is only a little lake, anyway, and this not to scoff at his experience, but to put the thing in some perspective) and never missed an opportunity of embellishing the story of how he, one day, came upon a rigid canoe lying in the reeds of the lake. For myself, I am chary of rigid canoes since the day I capsized in one in calm water. I was left hanging underwater for an uncomfortable time until I managed to wriggle out, and in so doing barked my shins so severely on the coaming that I was lucky to reach the shore by swimming, almost without the use of my legs. But they have their devotees, who swear by them.

But my hero 'borrowed' the rigid canoe and disporting himself out in the middle of the lake (your true storyteller, it is always the 'middle of the lake', nothing ever happens to him near the edge) was thoroughly enjoying himself under the full noon, strumming away on his guitar and carolling serenades to the stars, when he felt his pants growing cold and clammy.

Looking down, he beheld the canoe filling rapidly with water, and proceeded to make frantic efforts to paddle ashore. But his borrowed boat suddenly gurgled away from underneath, leaving him to struggle to the bank with the remains of the guitar. I was supposed to be awed into acquiescence by this tale, when it came to picking our trip. And I was. And of course, we were to have lakes for our first trial on open water.

We chose the Royal Canal, that practically disused waterway that flows out of Lough Owel in Westmeath, by Mullingar, Moyvalley, Enfield, Kilcock, Leixlip (where it is carried over the River Liffey), Lucan and Dublin city, where it flows into the Liffey at the North Wall; and we decided to continue the trip from Lough Owel by a little river into Lough Iron, thence by the River Inny to Lough Derravaragh, and by the Inny again to Loughs Kinale and Sheelin.

These lakes looked very small on the map. But I have since learned to treat maps with more respect. A lake from the bottom of a canoe looks quite a different proposition from the harmless little splash it makes on a half-inch Ordnance map.

So, one bright and sunny June day we set off for Blanchardstown, a few miles out of the city, to commence the journey. This starting point avoided the city stretches of the canal and a number of close-lying locks. We travelled in a friend's car and just as we were ready to say goodbye to him, I missed the tent. A nice pickle we would have been in the first night out without this essential! We constrained our obliging friend to run back to Dublin for it.

And so, with our roof, our food, our stove, our bed, and all other necessities that man requires for survival – whether travelling in the Arctic, the Equator, or on a humble canal –

stowed fore and aft in our little craft, we pushed off to commence our travels. In your collapsible there is an open cockpit about seven feet long and a decked space of about six feet forward and five feet aft. Under the decked ends the gear is stowed and you can stay out for a year if you feel like it, provided you have planned ahead for provisions. Usually we carried food and supplies for about three days.

We were most fortunate in our weather for this trip, striking a heatwave which lasted most of the time we were out. June, indeed, is one of the best months for a canoe trip, as well for the heat and the sun as for the long nights, for it stays bright almost until midnight. Being tyros, we worked to a too-well planned schedule. For we had the whole trip divided up, separated and dovetailed into a series of inhumanly equal distances, each of about twenty miles. This, though, allowed for halts of two or three days occasionally at good camping spots. Luckily, for we stuck to this diabolical plan through sun and wind, current and smooth water, rain and shine, in a way that almost finished my enthusiasm once and for all. However, it was but our first trip. Later we learned sense.

The canal was very pleasant. At times the banks rose steeply on each side, then again, one drifted through wide open meadows, or through the wooded estates of a demesne. We were away from the highways and as one gradually drew away from the city suburbs into the open country, a change could be noticed in the people met. For the country people of this quiet land seemed to have escaped the turmoil of modern life and to be a backwater of humankind that were more in keeping with the old sedate days of the passenger barges, the famous 'Fly Boats', that dragged their leisurely way through these quiet stretches in the early 1800s. Though from their title one can see that in those days they were considered to be the last word in speed on an inland waterway. In the canoe, in this easy water, twenty miles a day could be covered without effort. More, if ease were to be sacrificed to a definite goal.

Of course, there were portages. For the first ten miles these were constant enough. It meant alighting, but as we were young and strong, we thought little of heaving the canoe up to the higher levels without unpacking. Only in the sections where the banks were exceptionally steep did we unpack. We preferred any physical exertion spent in lifting *Minny* above the locks to the chore of unpacking and re-stowing.

I believe, for a nominal sum, one can have the locks filled to allow passage for a small boat. But our expenses were cut very fine and again, we were, in a sense, trespassing on the waters of the Royal Canal. We had, before setting out, made an effort to secure permission from the company to canoe on their canal. This permission had been refused on the simple grounds that the company would not be responsible for any accidents that might occur to us. Our naive attempt to declare that we would not claim in the event of our being drowned was politely turned down. But as we had no intention of having our cherished trip abandoned for such a piffling reason, we ignored the little tin gods and borrowed their canal. But the last thing we wanted was traffic with lock-keepers.

The first few lock-keepers we met immediately asked for our permit. In desperation we made them a story of having left it behind and being quiet men and not easily troubled they let us go without hindrance. Not so the inquisitive inspector who popped up on his bicycle after our second day. He too, appeared to believe the tale of the permit, but disappeared in the direction of Dublin and head office, with less credulity than we had believed.

Coming towards Maynooth we happened upon a stretch of excessively weeded water. For some miles the fine grass-like substance stretched from bank to bank and it was difficult to believe, in viewing the perspective, that there was a canal there at all. It proved arduous work digging the paddles into the stringy green mess. It was like being towed over an even, close-cropped lawn. I had believed that there was some little traffic on the canal, but the condition of this stretch would certainly belie it. It seemed a sad waste to see this fine inland waterway, laid down at immense pains and expense, falling into disuse and decay; especially so during the war years when transport laboured under unparalleled difficulties owing to lack of fuel. We saw a rare horse-drawn barge crawling along with its load of turf and this was the limit of the traffic. The railway, which had killed it, ran almost beside it, the whole way to Mullingar.

At Kilcock we drew ashore for dinner, making a good meal of potatoes, bacon and cabbage, at a very moderate price. This is a clean, neat little village and this day, in the brilliant sunshine which threw long shadows on its quiet streets, it was a nest of peace. In the main street we met a solitary gypsy woman who asked us for alms. She was tall and comely, her face tanned to a dark satin, her teeth brilliant and even, her eyes alive and laughing. She spoke in a rich sing-song brogue, showering blessings on us for our largesse. For we were in high humour, and bestowed generously.

Above Kilcock we made another portage and then settled down to enjoy the luxury of almost twenty miles of lock-free travelling, for we were now passing through the rich plains of royal Meath. We trailed a spinner behind and in this way we took turns to rest at the fishing. One would paddle for an hour, the other, feet dangling lazily over the coamings, stretched out at leisure. The line trailed behind and an occasional temerarious perch would be hauled aboard to wriggle and slither about the floor until his quietus came. The perch were of a fair size and we scaled them by dipping them in boiling water for a minute or two and fried them later in butter. They are excellent fare thus cooked and as the rivers and lakes of Ireland abound with them, we wondered why some enterprising businessman, say a returned American, had not attempted to catch them in the mass and can them.

We caught no pike and I was disappointed. Here and there throughout the trip, we were told hair-raising tales, especially in the local pubs, of monster fish that lurked in the canal, until one would be nervous even of canoeing in it. Once we saw a pike resting on the bottom holding a perch by the belly in his mouth, like a small boy with a large slice of bread. He lay motionless as we passed, to finish his dinner in peace. One hears tales also, of the weird assortments discovered in the rapacious bellies of these fish. Frogs, ducklings, watches, spoons and the like are sometimes met with. It is not without cause that it is sometimes known as the 'fresh-water shark'. Even in this country they grow to a great size and specimens weighing thirty pounds are not uncommon. In Lapland and Russia they have been caught measuring eight feet in length.

The term jack-pike refers to specimens of three pounds and under, or less than two feet in length. Pike bones are particularly dangerous to swallow, having the unpleasant property of not dissolving in the stomach, as do the small bones of most other fish.

There are many ways of cooking this fish, but imagine to yourself the flavour of a pike cooked according to the ritual of old Isaak Walton:

First open your pike at the gills, and if need be, cut also a little slit towards the belly. Out of these take his guts, and keep his liver, which you are to shred very small, with thyme, sweet marjoram, and a little winter savoury; to these put some pickled oysters and some anchovies, two or three, both these last whole, for the anchovies will melt and the oysters should not; to these you must add also a pound of sweet butter, which you are to mix with the herbs that are shred, and let them all be well salted.

If the pike be more than a yard long, then you may put into these herbs more than a pound, or if he be less, then less butter will suffice. These being thus mixed with a blade or two of mace, must be put into the pike's belly; and then his belly so sewed up as to keep all the butter in the belly if possible; if not, then, as much as you possibly can. But take not off the scales. Then you are to thrust the spit through his mouth, out at his tail. And then take four, or five, or six split sticks or very thin laths, and a convenient quantity of tape or filleting; these laths are to be tied around about the pike's body from his head to his tail, and the tape tied somewhat thick, to prevent his breaking, or falling off from the spit. Let him be roasted very leisurely, and often basted with claret wine, and anchovies and butter mixed together, and also with what moisture falls from him into the pan.

When you have roasted him sufficiently, you are to hold under him, when you unwind or cut the tape that ties him, such a dish as you propose to eat him out of, and let him fall into it, with the sauce that is roasted in his belly, and by this means the pike will be kept unbroken and complete. Then, to the sauce which was within, and also that sauce in the pan, you are to add a fit quantity of the best butter, and to squeeze the juice of three or four oranges. Lastly, you may either put it into the pike, with the oysters, two cloves of garlic, and take it whole out when the pike is cut off from the spit; or, to give the sauce a *haut gout*, let the dish into which you let the pike fall be rubbed with it; the using or not using of this garlic is left to your discretion. This dish of meat is too good for any but anglers, or very honest men; and I trust you will prove both, and, therefore, I have trusted you with this secret.

It would be recommended to rise early on the morning of preparation of such a sacrifice.

We passed through Moyvalley and made camp near the Hill of Down. When the tent was pitched and preparations for supper were in progress, the ubiquitous inspector again arrived and continued his questioning about our mythical permit. We, with difficulty, fobbed him off with embellishments on our former story. He was again going to Dublin in the morning and informed us that be would check up on the details. He was beginning to take the whole matter much too seriously for our liking. This character, who could no more mind his own business then I could cook Isaak's pike, was becoming a gadfly, raising wicked desires in the heart and profanities to the tongue. It was obvious something would have to be done about him. His type was rare in the country places, where they have a fine human disregard of petty, niggling regulations such as the one that was annoying us. We joked to ourselves about him, but his malign influence sat like an incubus on our dreams and we were astir early in the morning.

We walked after breakfast into the little village of the Hill of Down. Anything more peaceful and rustic it would be difficult to imagine. Overhead the hazed blue ceiling of heaven, unmarred by a solitary cloud, around us the level meadows and tilled fields, below the little humped bridge, the clear water of the canal in which fish could be seen darting amongst the yellow reeds; and the dusty little road leading into the village, which basked in the hot June sun, to all appearances uninhabited. We drank our beer at the counter of the pub, gazing through the wide open door at the lazy scene and listened in a torpor of contentment to our host's story of another monstrous pike which had been caught beneath the bridge.

On the way back it was decided to take leave of our unwelcome inspector, for we were reasonably certain that the pest would turn up to call our bluff and order us ignominiously off his canal. We deemed a silent withdrawal the more gracious thing and so we dismantled the canoe, packed all our camping gear and took the train from the tiny station to the town of Mullingar. Also, truth to tell, we were a little tired of the safety and humidity of the canal and were growing restless for our first lake that we might test *Minny* on the more boisterous waters of Lough Owel.

At Mullingar, having again assembled the canoe, (it's a wonderful advantage, this property of a collapsible – that it can be shut up like a suitcase if you change your mind and decide to make for distant territory) we started along the little feeder which supplies the canal with its water out of Lough Owel. It is a diminutive waterway and our large double-paddles had to be 'broken' into singles; and even these hardly had room enough to sweep. Here and there tiny foot-bridges spanned the feeder, so low that they looked like culverts from our approach. To negotiate them it was necessary to lie almost flat on the bottom and propel *Minny* along by pushing on the roof. Evidently the builders had never envisaged traffic of our kind on their little canal. In this way we came to the deep lock below the lake and anxiously scrambled up to take a look at our first lake.

It was not heartening, that first look. Remember we had been travelling on a waterway that seldom exceeded thirty feet in breadth and about six or seven feet in depth on average. It also enjoyed the tranquillity of the proverbial mill-pond. In addition, owing to the shelter of its banks and trees it contained the heat of the day and our lowness in the water warded off what mild breezes might blow. But Lough Owel was some miles across, a lot more than six feet deep, (it could have been a mile for all we knew; but we knew one could be drowned without a fuss in it) and was in a dirty humour when we saw it first. A powerful wind blew across the lake, whipping the surface into short angry waves and far out lines of white-caps gave warning that now indeed we might have opportunity to see what a collapsible canoe would stand in rough water. A small island stood about a mile out, its trees bent like rods drawing heavy catches.

Benny turned to me and shouted through the wind, 'You know, we could go back to Mullingar: the canal goes on to Termonbarry on the Shannon.' I tried weakly to grin.

'It's a bit rough, eh? Not a bit like those nice calm lakes on the tourist brochures,' I replied. 'I never thought they got up like this.'

'Well,' Benny answered, 'we are here now and this wind looks to be settled. We might as well get drowned today as next week in Sheelin. As a little matter of interest, did you know that Lough Sheelin is two or three times as big as Lough Owel?'

This was the big-lake navigator talking. I had intended to suggest that we wait awhile to see if the gale would drop, but as the hero walked cooly back to the canoe and commenced unpacking, I made a wry face at the windy lake and determined to try a fall with it.

We lifted *Minny* over the lock walls and placed her on the grass near the lake shore. Just at this point the water was at its roughest. The wind drove the water into the lock opening with great force and, apart from the splashing of breaking waves, a swell lifted the waters several feet. It did not seem possible to launch a canoe here and yet it was the only spot, for this shore was fringed with rocks.

We made preparations for lake weather. Here I bless the genius that designed the all-purpose rectangular cape-groundsheet. It is a garment of many uses. You sleep over it in the tent, you drape yourself from head to heel with it in wet weather and we found a new use for it more important even than these. An open canoe in rough water is about as safe as a tub and the folding canoe is consequently supplied with spray cover designed to cover in completely the open cockpit. These covers fit tightly, leaving only a small aperture for the body and they make the craft completely waterproof. The model of the folding canvas canoe is the Eskimo kayak, which is constructed of sealskin drawn over a wooden frame and having only the opening for the canoeist in its otherwise covered frame. The kayak is a most remarkable sea boat in the hands of an expert, capable of riding extremely heavy seas in safety. For some reason no spray cover had been available with our canoe when we purchased it, so we developed a method of lashing the two groundsheets around the coaming, leaving one corner loosely tied to a wing-nut for emergencies.

This makeshift cover proved extraordinarily strong and waterproof and indeed, (taking into consideration the really rough weather we afterwards ran into on the big lakes,) but for it, it would have been impossible to make the journeys we did without taking suicidal chances. A canoe being so low in the water and having an inside depth of only one-and-a-half feet, would be swamped by even one fair-sized wave.

So, with considerable care and not without trepidation, we pushed out into this new element, our little boat rising and diving like a cork. It was with a little anxiety that we saw her plunge her bow deep into the ragged combers, rising rapidly to shake off the spills which ran down to the peak of the cock-pit. As we slowly moved out from the shore it became evident that this was easy work for *Minny*. Funny the pride you take in a small boat when you are sure she is within her measure in coping with rough water. We fell in love with her after we had travelled about half a mile, and watched her dip and shake, roll and plunge like any old sea cow through the brave white-caps. Only then it was that we realised how dull the hours had been spent in the vacuum of the canal.

When we drew into Church Island (every lake in Ireland has an island or even two, called 'Church Island') our craft was, for the first time, drenched from stem to stern. But underneath our improvised covers we were dry and warm, not a drop had seeped through. We nosed in on the lee shore among tall reeds and Benny landed to explore the place while I lay back to smoke.

When an hour had passed without sign of his return, I went ashore to seek him out. The sun shone brilliantly, but the wind still blew strongly and waves pounded on the windward shore with a muffled sound. The island was mostly bog, with rowan and thorn trees speckled on its marshy surface. It was very low-lying. I cupped my hands and yelled Benny's name, but the wind carried the sound away. Finding a tall ash tree, I shinned up it to obtain a better view of the island. The wind almost blew me out of it, but a fair distance off I saw a patch of white. I immediately took it for the prone form of my companion, as we both wore white cotton jackets. I made for it at a trot, falling several times into bog-holes and discovered to my disgust that it was a large patch of marguerites. Heaven knows how they had ever came to grow in this lonely place. I pushed forward to the furthest extremity of the island, which was ringed in rowan trees and to my relief, beheld my friend in the distance. I had no stomach to push back across the lake alone, with a corpse or invalid for ballast.

The rowan clump proved to be a sort of miniature Everglades. The lake had encroached for many hundreds of yards among the boles and Benny, stupidly wandering among them, had got so far out that he was unable to find the track back. Together we discovered it and retraced our steps to the canoe.

We crossed the lake towards the south-west and here

discovered another peculiarity of lake navigation. You want to travel, say, from A to B. In theory it seems simple enough. One could make it as the crow flies, it seems. But if the crow travelled in a small boat it would find it quite a different matter. We started out, certainly, with our prow pointing straight for B. But after a few hundred yards we threw Euclid overboard, for we found that the shortest distance between two points, in a canoe, is the safest distance between those points. Mind you, in the deep books they write now on mathematics, which is being raised from a science to a theology, there is a very supercilious attitude taken towards poor old Euclid. The coming of the Theory of Relativity and all its train, has postulated the fourth dimension and consequent abstruse calculations and alas, that old rationalist, who haunted our youth, who walked on dry land, who measured things with his three-dimensional eyes; this solid man (and I mean no pun) is grown too simple for our modern mathematicians and has become a lecturer to children.

Knowing no better, we endeavoured to follow his age-old axiom, but alas it does not hold good on lakes. We could, no doubt, have found it well demonstrated in a big book on navigation, but like Euclid, we discovered it for ourselves. For an inland lake is like a woman and is a creature of caprice. You might head for a point a mile away, starting prow-on to the waves and though the wind may not change (or appear to change) you suddenly find large waves breaking over your beam, threatening you with capsizing. You are compelled to change course, for you must keep her head-on to the waves and in a little while, you have to change again. And this goes on. So that we reached the little rivulet out of Lough Owel, marked on our Ordnance map, in a series of crooked darts and dashes. This we discovered afterwards applied to all lakes, and discovered a great and fundamental truth about navigation that made us wiser men.

❧

The little blue ribbon that was to lead us from Lough Owel to Lough Iron proved an imposture. We had had a week of dry, burning weather and when we had followed this miserable stream for a hundred yards, we found that it dribbled away to a mere trickle of water that would scarcely float a cork. As we drew but four-and-a-half inches and had been sanguine that there was no river shown on a map that would be too shallow to bear us, we were sadly disappointed.

While we lay in about five inches of water, cursing the map and the map-makers, as is the wont of men who land themselves in trouble through their own negligence, two men approached us in a boat. They were both standing, one poling her along in the shallows, the other messing about with a fishing rod. They gazed upon *Minny* with eyes large in wonder. One could see at a glance that canoes were not a commonplace around here.

'That's a great little craft ye have there, men', said the man with the rod.

'Aye, she's a good little boat', one of us answered, feeling proud of our cockleshell.

'Where'd ye spring from now, if I might not be too inquisitive?'

'Oh,' nonchalantly, as if we did it every morning before breakfast, 'we came down from Dublin. Just crossed Owel, but we seem to have ended in a cul-de-sac. This stream dries up here and we had planned to reach Lough Iron by it.'

'D'ye mean to say ye crossed Lough Owel in *that*?'. The 'that' sounded very deprecatory and rather warmed us.

'Yes, certainly, it's only a small lake, y'know, and a canoe can take it easily.' How quickly experience is assimilated and made to look old.

'Well, bedambut, man, ye wouldn't find *me* crossing in it,

not for the sons of man, would you now, John?' This to the gilly, who grinned, shook his head, and vowed that the ground could open and swallow him, or the lake for that matter, before he would risk his precious person in such a flimsy yoke on the 'tracherous lake'. For Owel had a bad name with the residents on its shores.

We stayed gossiping awhile and asked if there was any outlet from the lake by which we might reach the River Inny. There was none. What, then, could we do to have our canoe and our effects taken to the river? Well, if we 'rowed' up to a certain point on the lake, we could walk some miles to a tradesman who had a lorry and who might hire us this for a reasonable sum. But it was 'chancey, chancey'. Then, very generously, he offered to take us, our canoe and all the equipment, to Inny by his own car. This was Irish hospitality and made us proud of our blood.

With much outward protestation and much inner thankfulness, we accepted. The car was a Ford Eight. We lashed *Minny* to the roof, stowing the bags and pots inside and reached the River Inny in half an hour, cutting out Lough Iron. Generous man! May he have his reward for this charity.

The Inny was a brown, quiet river, as befitted one that lived mostly in a bog. For the two days we spent on it we saw nothing but interminable bog and marshland on both banks. Also, the river was aptly named, for Inny is a corruption of the Irish *Inigeacht* – crooked. It twisted like a brown snake through the reeds and thorn trees of its banks in such a way that after several miles, the landmarks which at one time were on your right hand, turned up on your left; those that had been directly behind, appeared mysteriously in front; and the distant mountains 'skipped like rams'. Neither did they recede on our approach, but seemed always to stay at an equal distance, so that sometimes we wondered if our progress had been illusory. A strange river, the Inny.

We found a carpet of lush, short grass on the edge of a copse and late in the evening we pitched camp. The loneliness and silence of the spot is memorable. Rarely have I halted in a more solitary place. As far as the eye could reach, on either bank was bog and whins, broken with turf-ricks at irregular intervals. A lone figure might sometimes be seen in the distance loading a cart with the fuel. On each hand the river wound quickly out of sight around its innumerable bends. Behind the camp a few hungry trees broke the level of the bog. It was a haunt of great numbers of wild fowl. When the sun sank on the western ridge of the wood, splaying his last weak rays among the purple heavens, they winged over the bog to the sedges and mudflats of the river: mallard, tern and black-backed gull, plover, teal, curlew and snipe came to their feeding-ground in the last light.

Round the comfort of the camp fire after dinner, we lay and talked and I relished the luxury of the late pipe. About us was blackness. The harsh quack of a restless duck sounded in the night, but the leaping flames and the pale outline of the tent were our refuge from the mystery of the unknown place, for it was an eerie spot at night and I do not doubt that, if one had a mind for it, ghosts could be raised by the pair on that bald, pool-pocked plain. But we were quiet men and let them rest, hoping they would keep faith with us.

Under the warm morning sun we bathed in the bog-river before breakfast. Later, as we passed silently along, we marvelled at the plenty of game. Every turn of that ever-turning river brought us into a flock of wild duck that scattered madly when we appeared. The canoe is a very silent thing and we arrived on top of them without creaking of oars or squealing of rowlocks. Had we a shotgun we could have killed enough for the trip. Only in one other place, a little lake called Coalpit in Co Cavan, have I seen more wild duck gathered together. Filled more with the romance of an inland voyage through lovely country than the desire to feed at all costs on bird flesh, we came armed only with a small four-foot hunting bow and a few arrows. It was more ornamental than useful and as the arrows were expensive and home-made ones difficult to make, we were compelled to chase into outlandish places to retrieve them. As we both were beginners the fowl were in less danger than ourselves. But it was a galling thing to see those flocks of wild duck, plover and snipe thick as bees round your head and know that, try as you might, you still would have to fall back on tinned beans and stewed steak. We rarely had fresh meat. It would not keep twelve hours in the heat and we required to carry provisions for two days, as shops were rare.

The Inny finds its way out of Lake Derravaragh in an unobtrusive way and we were approaching upstream. We noticed that the river had gradually widened, the flow was negligible and great islands of reed appeared scattered on the water. The banks gradually disappeared behind wide fringes of more reeds, growing to a height of five or six feet. In my ignorance I thought we were already in the lake and was not prepared for the wonderful scene that appeared to us as we emerged quite suddenly through a veritable meadow of reeds onto the placid waters of the lake.

We faced the northern extremity of Lough Derravaragh, which stretched for miles to the south-east, ending in a high, green, beautifully rounded hill at this extremity. The lake is shaped like the letter 't', with a gradual tapering from the horizontal part of the letter. We had entered from the extreme corner of the cross-piece and the lake stretched away on our right hand for two or three miles. The shores were heavily wooded, especially the southern shore, the banks rising in a series of low, rolling hills on each side of the valley that held the lake like a turquoise in this emerald setting. The sun was shining brilliantly, there was no wind, the lake was unruffled, even the trees on the nearest shore to us stood tall and silent and, in fact, it was just such a picture as I had always imagined of a lake. And a rare enough one to came across in reality, as later experience proved.

As we glided along by the woods over clear water, that revealed the golden sand in its shallows, such a peace came over me as is rarely vouchsafed to the man condemned to live out his life in cities. It was a deep, tremendous restfulness that flowed into the soul from this scene of the majesty of nature, that spoke to one with the mystery of things created and made communion between the sentient and insensate, as works of the one great mind. Easy it was in this great peace to see birds and trees and animals as fellow creatures, not to be abused and maltreated because they are beneath us, but to see in them the friendliness of our common existence and dependence, as the Beggar of Assisi did, who called them his brothers. But this is a great and secret grace and not often given to men.

We drew ashore about half way down the lake on the right bank and pitched camp in a glade among the woods, about two hundred yards from shore. There in the evening after a meal, (for we did not live to a breakfast-dinner-tea routine as in the city; we broke fast well enough in the morning, took another meal when hungry – one might call it dinner, for it would be a huge meal in which every sort of eatable went into the pot – and nothing, or another great feed, at night, as the humour took us) there, I say, after a meal, we sat on a ridge covered in coarse ferns, buried under the foliage of the trees and gazed out over the lake that now was a very epitome of peace and beauty and evening. It was a singularly silent lake and in the few days that we spent on its shores, we beheld but two boats. One was an eel fisherman's, the other was a kind of barge affair that drew timber from one end of the lake to a sawmill at the other end. It seemed that this crude craft was specially designed to equilibrate the silence that held Derravaragh like a spell all day.

For it made a monstrous noise with its ungainly outboard motor and chugged back and forth throughout the day, luckily at long intervals, but the roar of the engine was heard all along the lake shores, for sound travels far over still water.

Derravaragh is a storied lake. It was the setting of one of the loveliest and tenderest of the old Irish legends, the enchantment of the Children of Lir. For it was at Derravaragh, (the lake of the little oak wood) that Aoife cast the spell on her four step-children, changing them into four snow-white swans and dooming them, by virtue of her gift of sorcery as a queen of the fairy people, to nine hundred years in that form. Three hundred years of the spell were to be spent on Derravaragh, three hundred on the Strait of Moyle and three hundred on the Atlantic coast. The children retained the gift of human speech and of music, the latter considered always a special gift of the Danann and by the shores of the lake, for the first period of the spell, the Danann folk would gather to hear the exquisite singing and to converse with the enchanted children. When the nine hundred years were over and the requisites for the breaking of the spell fulfilled, the children of Lir were transformed in the presence of Deoca, a princess of Munster and her people, into their original human form, but now changed by the centuries into old, shrivelled and dying beings. They were baptised Christian, it was said, before death.

In the morning we walked across country to Multyfarnham. And here an amazing incident occurred. We had sadly become inured to the Irish country habit of staring at strangers, especially strangers like us, dressed in shorts, white jackets and berets, a dress stranger then than it is now. Also, our habit of arriving in a village or town as if from the blue sky – for in all but towns in a large and popular boating place, as at Athlone on the Shannon, river travellers are remarkably rare – made us more than ever an object of curiosity. But the reception in Multyfarnham, a pretty, forgotten little backwater nestling in well-wooded country, was the most bizarre of all. Firstly, every infant who could walk gathered around and furtively followed us up the main street. Then, as if at the call of a bugle, a gaggle of fat geese that had been standing by a cottage gate, idly gossiping, marched out ceremoniously into the middle of the street and joined in the procession. Stopping when we stopped, turning when we turned, the Inquisitive Geese of Multyfarnham were not to be put off and insisted on escorting us a considerable distance through the village, until we panicked and fled into the nearest grocery store. There, in the street outside, they stood in line like a platoon on parade, awaiting our return. Poor birds, I wonder how long they had to wait before again they had such a public holiday.

A surprise awaited us at camp. We found two hardy-looking fellows sitting outside the tent, brewing tea on the embers of our camp fire. At first we thought we had surprised a pair of wanderers making themselves at home with our provisions, but they turned out to be eel fishermen, brothers, whom we had met on the Inny some days before. They were fishing the lake and kindly invited us to join them that night. We jumped at the opportunity, but our enthusiasm dropped a little when they told us they did not go out until 3 a.m. However, one such early rising would not kill us. We lit a great fire of dead wood and the four of us turned in about 11 p.m., for the tent was roomy and at a squeeze could have accommodated five or six.

They awoke us in the darkness and we made a cup of tea before starting out, to offset the chill of the night air. It was bitterly cold as we boarded their long, beamy boat and a wind with the breath of the frozen north in it blew over the lake.

Their method of fishing was this. They let out a line baited at intervals with worm, minnow or such small fish. Sometimes, too, artificial bait would be used. This line was suspended from floats and ran for a mile or so in a straight line, well out in the lake, then it turned and ran up the lake, turned again and down, and so on, until a great area was covered.

It was weird there in the darkness, under the stars that glistened like ice-flakes, to move slowly and quietly over the still waters, watching the fishermen pulling up the baited cross-lines, to toss the catch into the well of the bottom. One is not at all sure what will be found on the hooks and along with the eels, large perch and pike were pitched into the squirming, wriggling mass that splashed around our feet. The eels, indeed, seemed at home there, and swam up and down under the footboards in an inch or two of water that was left there purposely to keep them alive. For they are not killed but packed alive in ice and shipped off to England, mainly to Billingsgate. A good price is paid for them and they net a tidy sum for the shipper, who often is a small farmer using this sideline as a paying one.

We saw the dawn break over the tops of the trees and a stronger wind arose that whipped up sharp, choppy little wavelets. With the spray from these and the splashing from innumerable eels, that made one feel as if sitting in a boat whose bottom was alive, we got decently wet. The catch, we were told, was very poor, and they said that this lake once had been an eel fisher's paradise, but for some mysterious reason, year by year the yield grew smaller. We spoke of the wonderful story of the eels' migrations: how all eels are hatched in the Sargasso Sea, that vast floating area of weed that covers a gigantic triangular patch of the central Atlantic Ocean; how they make their blind way, first as larvae, then as elvers, finally as full-grown eels to the fresh water habitat of the parents; how they wriggle in the night over fields to quarries and ponds, as well as finding their way to lakes and rivers; how they live there for years, until one day the instinct that drew them there sends them off again on the immense journey homeward to the Sargasso Sea, there to breed, and die. It is only in recent years that this great mystery of the eel has been discovered through the research of a famous Danish oceanographer, Dr Schmidt, who spent years in the study of this strange fish and so solved the puzzle of why you never find the eggs of the eel in fresh water or how they mysteriously appear overnight in places where it was known that they had not been before.

When we arrived at the camp we made a remarkably big breakfast, as we were cold and shivering. We went to bed and slept till midday.

Later that day the noisy barge came chugging close to our shore and drew in on the beach where the canoe was drawn up. Apparently the occupants were as interested in *Minny* as we were in their monster of noise, for we found them standing by her, gazing in unfeigned wonder on her frail form. They were two nice young fellows and plied us with questions about the canoe: Where was it made? Of what was it constructed? Was it safe? Did we ever capsize? Spring a leak? and a hundred others. They had never seen anything like it and like the gillie on Lough Owel, 'Wouldn't put a foot in it fur a forchun.' It was amusing the way they kept repeating, 'Well it's a fret, surely.'

'Fret' was the colloquialism for 'fright' and like the 'Tarra' of the North, could be used as a superlative for the most contradictory things. Perhaps a little tale will illustrate this, a tale popular in Armagh during the time the American troops were stationed in the North.

An American soldier of the acquisitive type, who 'collected' pithy sayings from different countries and districts, was greatly puzzled by the catholic use of the word 'tarra', as 'terror' is pronounced in the North. This word is used indiscriminately there in every conceivable context, so that the American could make neither head nor tail of it; for of course he didn't recognise the word as 'terror', though even if he had, it would not have helped him.

'How is it,' he one day asked an old greybeard that he met in a village pub, 'that when I meet a man in this country and I say to him, "That's a fine warm day," that he answered, "Och, sure, it's a tarra"? And again, I meet another man, and I say to him "That's a cold, bad day," and he likewise answers, "Och, it's a tarra." And, indeed, no matter what I say, somebody will put in, sooner or later, "Aye, it's a tarra." Now, my gracious man, I am interested in dialect and colloquialisms, and for my peace of mind, explain to me what is the meaning of this word "tarra", for you look an intelligent fellow, and your grey hairs speak wisdom.'

And the Northman answered, 'And d'ye mean to tell me ye don't know what "tarra" means? D'ye really mean to tell me that?'

'I sure do.'

'Well,' said the old man, as he finished his glass, and wiped the froth off his stubble with the back of his hand, 'that's a tarra to the world of God!' And, like the wise old man that he was, he knew that he had explained it adequately.

Later that day we decided to visit the green hill that lay at the southern end of the lake. It was a hill of singular beauty, rising out of the lake shore gloriously symmetrical and round, and of a most vivid green. We had been wondering about it for days and conjectured that it must certainly be the Rath of the Árd Rí of the Sídhe. So we decided to introduce ourselves and set off on fine calm water under a blazing sun. Apparently the Árd Rí didn't like visitors, for we had gone but a mile towards it when the sky grew dark, a few heavy drops fell and a cold biting wind sprang up. It was typical of these inland lakes that in about ten minutes it was blowing a fresh breeze, a shower of hailstones hammered off the canoe and we were drenched with the spray of the waves and the hail. We had brought no spray sheets and as we were clad only in bathing shorts it was not a pleasant experience. We raced for the shore paddling like madmen and cursing better. We perforce had to shelter for an hour, utterly miserable, under the trees and listened with a wooden apathy to the peals of thunder that broke over our heads.

Then, as suddenly as it began, the gale ceased and in a few minutes the sun broke through again, the lake assuming its innocent mirror-like appearance. But we took a last look at the inviting hill and left it there, returning to camp to brew tea as hot and strong as the can would hold.

Our awakening next morning was a little unusual. We were startled from our sleep by a thudding and the twanging of guy-ropes. We awoke simultaneously and stared at each other. Then, Benny, springing out of bed in his shirt, (a sports shirt, not reaching to his backside) shouted, 'Cattle', and disappeared through the door-flaps like a disturbed satyr. There was a loud howling and banging and 'shoo-ing' outside and hastily following, I beheld him, like Hercules holding the Giants at bay, dancing here and there amongst a large herd of cattle and dealing out, with a lavish hand, hefty thumps and thwacks on buttock and nose with a paddle-blade. I took part in the game and we dispelled then amongst the trees with a loud crashing of branches. All, that is, except one. For when we had chased the herd, this great brute, a magnificent looking animal, still stood but a few yards from the tent, gazing with an absorbed interest at its appurtenances. Never was there such an inquisitive fauna as the fauna of this district. Maybe it was the innocence of animals which little knew man, as explorers of Tibet and other places have reported astonishing tameness in animals that were strangers to man, maybe there was a *genius loci* of curiosity in the place, but there the beast stood, unabashed at our shouting and banging, adamant. Benny dealt him a few lusty blows on the nose. He merely grunted and withdrew a pace, showing no sign of fear.

'What a gallus bullock,' my indignant partner cried, 'I declare to God I've never seen such impudence,' as we both stood back and stared at him.

'Are you sure he's a bullock?' I asked.

'What else can he be? You don't suppose it's a cow or a heifer?'

Something struck him suddenly and he walked off at a tangent to examine closer. He came back at a trot.

'Quick. Get the tent down. Don't touch him. Gather up everything as quickly as you can. Don't make too much noise.'

The staccato sentences told me all I wanted to know. It was a bull, without a doubt. A young one, but very big. We dived on the pegs and in a shameful panic, threw the tent flat on the ground, piling onto it everything moveable around the place. Our interested ox snorted softly and commenced to paw the earth. We gathered the four corners of the tent as a lazy housewife might clear a table and half-ran with our bulky bundle towards the beach. The bull followed at a trot. We ran. He gathered speed. Finally we reached the canoe and had her in the lake, loading furiously. One of us waded out, pushing her, the other warned off our companionable beast with stones. At which he grew mad and commenced to bellow, ending up by charging at us. In a flurry of foam and splashes we shot out on the lake, while the young bull pawed on the beach, lashing his tail and roaring for blood.

Having thus put out without breakfast and without pre-meditation, we found that the lake was very rough. Though the sun shone strongly, a stiff breeze stirred the waters into heavy waves. We ran as close to the shore as was consistent with safety, thus avoiding the worst of it, for the centre looked bad. As we drew towards the head of the lake, it became obvious that we could not cross the wide upper reach undecked, and we pulled ashore and affixed the spray-covers.

The Inny flows into the lake from the north and out again almost north-west, there being about two miles between influx and efflux. This river is the main feeder of the lake, which has only one other river flowing into it, the little Gaine. Some streams add their moiety from the eastern and southern shores, but the broad Inny fills this lush basin in an off-hand way, not flowing out at a point almost opposite to its influence, in the way a river usually fills a valley, but continuing purposely in its original direction to seek again the bare brown wastes of the bog.

We got our first baptism of rough water crossing Derravaragh. The waves seemed mountainous to us who viewed them from as low a point as is possible in any craft. *Minny* battled bravely along, shivering and creaking, gamely taking their rough handling without protest. The really big ones curved forward rapidly and swallowed her prow almost to the cockpit, then poured along the spray covers and the sides. We learned the trick of irregular paddling, easing the canoe forward gently in the milder waters and pushing her high on the big waves before they had time to break over us.

For some unknown reason I broke out into a roaring shanty in the middle of all this pother. It seemed a silly thing to do, as we were fully occupied endeavouring to get safely to the mouth of the river. But I so enjoyed the thrill and tension of the crossing, that some justice had to be done to the little boat and though at that hour I never so considered it, I sang for her. Just then I sang because I wanted to sing, but no doubt there was a reason for it. For, God help me, I was new to the game, new to the lakes and new to rough water and a bucking boat. I took it calmer afterwards in much bigger lakes and rougher water, when I certainly did not feel like singing. But now I had found my wings and chirruped for glee.

So we came once more to calm water and our crooked bog-river; a friendly river, despite its lonely habitat. We pulled up below Float bridge and walked to the village of Coole, to fill our provision bags.

Some miles beyond, near a townland with the mellifluous name of Derreenamaddoo, which is obviously but a slight corruption of the Irish name and probably means 'the little wood of the fox', we pitched camp. It was here that we saw the two cuckoos. A pleasant green place it was, with thickets of whitethorn and elder and all about a carpet of fine grass, like the best lawn grass, covered the ground. It looked like a habitation from which the house had been mysteriously spirited away, leaving not a trace and the gardens and lawns had slowly and reluctantly fallen back to nature's careless hand.

We explored it separately, wandering about for hours before we met. In the trees sang the two cuckoos. Heavy, unbalanced birds, they laboured from tree to tree in an ungainly flight, the long drooping tails making it appear that they had the greatest difficulty in staying awing. All the time they sang. Their hollow two-tone notes sparkled over the little oasis, emphasising the harmony of green grass and brown high-reeded river; emphasising too, the loneliness of the bare and colourless bog. I knew then what this burgeoning meant to our fathers, before the coming of public lighting, electricity, hot and cold running-water, radios, a plenitude of books and the amenities that now make a winter bearable. Coming out of their short cold days and long black nights, they hailed the rising sap and the waxing sun, heralded in the soft song of the cuckoo, as in the earliest of English lyrics,

Summer is i-comen in,
Loud sing cuckoo;
Groweth seed and bloweth mead
And springeth the wood new.
Sing Cuckoo.
Loweth after calfe cow,
Bullock sterteth,
Buck verteth,
Merrie sing cuckoo.
Cuckoo, Cuckoo;
Well thou singest cuckoo.
Nor cease thou never now.

'Nor cease thou never now.' Such a heartfelt longing. Now the strong sun and a blue sky, now the warm noon and the rich scent of woodbine, the bright splash of wild flowers. Now the long quiet days, the parturition bringing forth the summer child. How they must have longed for this and shouted the good news, the first cuckoo song, the promise that never failed, the lover's trysting note.

In this happiness we chose to pitch our tent and to remain on the pleasant island for three day. The peace of it and the contentment were too much to allow of either reading or writing. It was certainly suited to reflection or to the changeling of that virtue, the gazing into space while the mind dropped to a low level of half-formed thoughts, incomplete deductions and unfinished prognostications. A very pleasant state it is, this daydreaming, so akin to sleep; so sweet, when you are propped on a green bank with scattered thickets in front, peopled with singing birds, the sun lazing among cirrocumulus and a river chuckling behind you. On such days I endeavoured to read from my little anthology, choosing the fitting verse:

'The flowers appear on the earth;

The time of the singing of birds is come...'

But the mind lost the thread quickly and dropped to its lazy bottom saying, 'Why look in books for what you have around you?' As Stevenson has truly said, 'Literature is a fine thing, but it is no substitute for life.' I would take the bow and the one good arrow and wander off among the low trees to hunt a rabbit, or take the canoe and drive a mile or two upstream, towing the spinner to catch a fish, and relishing the drift back without any movement. This drifting became a great pastime. For you could stretch out at ease in the empty canoe and in the most complete silence, with but a rare paddle touch, float down the river on your back. At least that is what it most nearly represented and you never got wet. Lotus-eating.

We left the friendly, lonely Inny and came to Lough Kinale, about one-and-a-half miles long by a mile wide. It is heavily fringed with reeds and connected to Lough Sheelin by a short stretch of the Inny. The county borders run through Lough Kinale, dividing the counties of Longford, Westmeath and Cavan. We saw on the shore of the lake as wild looking a habitation as might ever have been seen in the days of the rack-renters and the potato famine. It was a mud cottage, standing on barren, rock-strewn land, a goat grazing by the gable end, beside a rain-barrel. The cottage itself was dirty and decayed, the thatched roof collapsed, smoke spiralling upward through the gaps. As we looked, a wild-looking woman, her hair hanging in straight, unkempt locks, opened the half-door and glared at us for several minutes. She ignored our waved greeting, re-entered the cottage and banged the half-door shut. A portent.

Perhaps if we had been superstitious we might have turned back.

It was very late in the evening when we came to Lough Sheelin. It looked enormous after Owel, but then, as remarked before, any sizeable lake does when viewed from the bottom of a canoe. Sheelin was not rough, but a strong wind blew across, lifting little rollers that ran rapidly towards the north-east shore. The sky was now clouding and it seemed that our Mediterranean weather, which had been with us with hardly a break for about ten days, was coming to an end.

Deciding to get well up the lake while the calm lasted, we paddled northwards up the centre. The impression of size was here further added to, for the shores on either hand were now dim in the grey light, the surrounding hills alone holding a glimmer on their summits. It was a dark, sullen lake that did not like strangers. A lake you would not trust even on a fine day. It appeared to have few islands, in this being unlike the generality of Irish lakes, which are mostly peppered with them. One large island rose in the centre, but seemed to be the usual heavily wooded type, which often offer no campsites, owing to a dense undergrowth of thickets and nettles. We landed on a small island close to the north-east shore and after pitching tent in the dark, a lugubrious proceeding, we made supper and turned in. In bed we heard the wind rising and the lake worked itself to an ugly roar. The surf beat on the rocky shore with a dull, monotonous pounding, that lulled us to sleep.

When we rose next morning the good weather had gone, and with it the good temper of the lake. I stood on the shore, and gazed out over a restless, heaving sea of waters, huge, curling whitecaps that covered the full extent of the lake. They roared on the shingle at my feet, writhing forward amongst the curious rocks which had been eaten into strange shapes through centuries of the action of wind and water. It looked most dangerous and was totally unfit for canoeing, spray-sheet or no spray-sheet. The sky was basalt, unrelieved by light. The wind howled furiously, bending the thin starved trees surrounding our camp. They were rowans and must have been of great age. They bore a grey stubble of lichen all over, that gave them the semblance of an old, decrepit, unshaven man. Many were rotten from the roots up, all had withered branches. They grew in thickets that stretched out far into the shallows of the lake. It looked like a little wood that carried the shadow of a heavy curse.

During our stay on Sheelin we saw no sign of life; no boats on the lake, no movement on the shore. The next day, a comparative calm having fallen, we set off for the mainland, where we left the canoe, and trekked through the fields to the road. We walked to the village of Finnea, filled our provision bag and enjoyed the serenity of a quiet drink. The walk back, about four miles under great beeches and oaks, was excellent, stretching the legs after the confinement of the canoe.

That night I had the unpleasant experience of being awakened by a rat running across my legs. I woke up instantly, for out of doors I slept lightly. Benny also woke, and we poked around the tent with our torches looking for him, keeping our knives handy to deal with him. He had, however, made his escape, but left signs of his depredations on some of the foodstuffs. He was a particularly cheeky rat, as next day we saw him several times scampering around the tent and arrows and stones seemed not to annoy him. We often had heard rats scraping about outside the tent in different places, but this was the only one that had the temerity to explore inside. It was our habit to take the open foodstuffs inside the tent at night, leaving the tinned stuffs outside against the wall of the tent. The paddles too, were brought in, as they made good windbreaks at each end of the tent and were not in danger of being trampled to splinters by inquisitive cattle.

We spent the second-last day of the trip polishing our mud-caked shoes, washing our grimy shirts and socks, sewing torn shorts and jackets, and generally getting ready for the unwelcome return to civilisation. The wind was again blowing in strength (I often wondered how many windless days in the year these lakes were blessed with) and all day the breakers roared on the shore. Lough Sheelin never gave us much opportunity to explore it and we had perforce to abandon our proposed run to lonely Church Island.

The last evening we spent squatting around a great campfire, I smoking, Benny poking absently at the sizzling timber and both of us listening to the gale. We told ghost stories, the atmosphere of the place being so in keeping with our talk that we droned them in low monotones. As the wind showed no sign of abating that night, we agreed to rise at dawn, the one hour you are almost certain to find a lull in even the most consistent bad weather.

We conjectured rightly, for at six o'clock, the lake had dropped to a dead calm and the wind was down. We stole away without breakfast over the leaden waters and over an hour later we made our first meal by the safe shore of little Kinale. As if to have the last laugh, the sun rose in all his glory and under a great heat and stillness, we staggered through the fields, beneath the cumbersome paraphernalia of canoe bags, tent, haversacks, pots and pans, the perspiration streaming down our faces and our clothes clammily sticking to our steaming bodies.

At Ballywillan the bags went into the guard's van and in a few hours we were in Dublin.

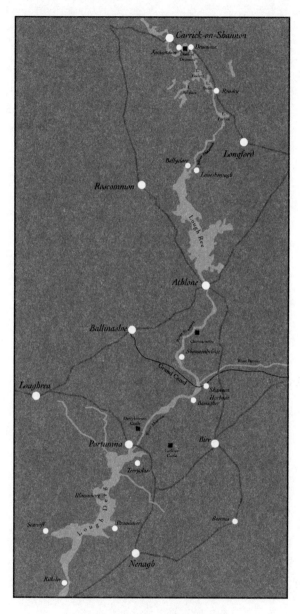

The Shannon and Lough Ree

THE SHANNON AND LOUGH REE

We commenced our Shannon trip at Carrick-on-Shannon. We could have began further north, at Lough Allen, for instance, which is a pretty lake. But as well as taking into consideration the overall length of the journey, (for we had determined to make Limerick our terminus) it was the nearest direct railhead.

So, after a most tedious train journey of ten hours, in which the fire in the engine gave out (for it was Emergency travel) and had to be drawn and re-lit at Multyfarnham, we reached Carrick. It was about eight o'clock in the evening when we arrived, bored beyond telling, and cramped beyond measure. Also, we were hungry as gulls. We had not eaten since seven in the morning, there being no restaurant car on this wild train. It was with a great prayer of thankfulness that I set about an enormous steak, a good inch thick, running blood and smothered with onions, in the Hotel something or other, which provided excellent fare for famished travellers.

It was fully ten o'clock, then, when we hired our 'gillies', as we jocosely termed the lads we pressed to carry our huge bags to the river. In this case, as the river was a fair distance away, the impediment went into a donkey-cart driven by a young urchin, his younger brother leading the flea-bitten quadruped. We sauntered in front, the wagon close behind, at least half the juvenile population of Carrick and their dogs bringing up the rear. In this way, like a safari reaching the Zambesi, we came to the lordly Shannon, the largest river in these islands. Even here it was a wide, slow, open river, gently moving, not a bit like our old tortuous friend, the Inny. You could see where you were going on the Shannon and where you had come from.

We built the canoe at a spanking rate, anxious to leave the purlieus of Carrick and its interested citizens behind. Then, just as the night came down, we pushed off with many a wave and cheer from the envious boys. When the church spire at Carrick was but a dim needle in the distance we hauled ashore and set up camp. It was midnight but it was June and quite light. The bright stars were out, in patience awaiting the final curtain of night and their lone vigil.

Not far below Carrick, the river opens into Lough Corry. This is properly not a lake at all, but one of those ample spreadings of the great river over low-lying land. We passed by Jamestown, a tiny place, but still retaining the remains of its ancient walls in the form of a fine arched gateway, for it once was a place of importance, having its own Council of Burghers and its charter given by James I. Beyond, we continued our quiet way by pleasant level meadows and still copses rustling in the sun, until we came to Drumsna, a sleepy little village but a stone's throw from the river. Cattle, standing up to their bellies in the water, owled at us as we drew ashore. We were low in provisions and had decided to replenish here. We were madly disillusioned. Drumsna had no bread, no meat, no tinned foods. The grim prospect at rationing our avid appetites or pushing on with all speed to Rooskey, was only partially alleviated by our purchases of eggs, potatoes and Oxo cubes. Had we been at the ballad-making school we might have outdone the famous diatribe of Fergus O'Byrne on Doneraile, where his watch was stolen.

Coming into Lough Boderg we were caught in a downpour of rain. From the uniform grey of the sky it was to last a good hour or more. We found a tall pole sticking out of the lake bottom near the reedy selvedge and to this hitching-post we moored the canoe. We lay down on the wooden flooring, pulling the spray cover over our heads and in this dark pit, lulled by the monotonous splashing of the rain, we dozed the shower away. We found our night rest on Rabbit Island in Lough Bofin, which is really a continuation of Lough Boderg.

Rooskey was far better provided with foodstuffs than unhallowed Drumsna. As it was the half-holiday we were limited to one shop, which presumably because they saw us coming, remained open. My diary shows the short, but telling, phrase, 'Excessive charge for foodstuffs.' How is it that certain conscienceless shopkeepers delight in battening on strangers, who pass their way but once. Maybe, this is why it is done. If a man sells to someone whom he expects to buy again, he will be cautious and unctuous to a degree. But the unfortunate traveller, who comes once to buy and pass silently on, is looked upon as a lamb specially led thither by the gods of grocers for fleecing.

We made portage around the lock at Rooskey and now were coming into the great Shannon plain, by the bare, low banks of which the river rolls in a dark, sluggish stream. For miles on either hand there is no break on the level horizons. Occasional cottages or farmhouses slowly swam into view, remained near in their solitariness for a little while and as slowly faded away again. Here was no lively twisting and frolicking, as was the way at the puckish Inny, no switching of landmarks from right to left, no jumping mountains, no illusion of making no way. This mighty river took itself seriously, stroked its patriarchal beard and spoke, 'You are on an ancient and hallowed highway. This way came from the North, the first peoples of your island; down to the plains rowed the fairy-folk of Dana and of Miled. After them, followers of Patrick, cenobite and mendicant, to found on my banks the Schools of the West. Later still, the wolfish Norseman, with torch and sword; and after him the Saxon, who dared come no further, for I sheltered with my broad bosom the hunted sons of Ireland, who fed on hate amongst the barren lands of Connaught. You will bear these things in your mind and travel without haste in a straight path. For I am no mountain stream, but move in majesty to the mighty ocean.'

It is without doubt that rivers have a character of their own and one that imbues the soul of the voyager with their peculiar spirit. For on the Shannon you travel easily and in a kind of awe. There is no need of haste; there is no dawdling either, for there is little of interest on the river itself. Only on the big lakes may one potter about among islands and ruined abbeys and the crumbling shells of castles.

But here the slow and lazy river gave no sound, the only evidence of its movement might be a twirling leaf or steady straw, infinitesimal things on the broad green breast, moving like puppets of fate to the Unknown. One could not but be affected by such benign indifference.

The next lake, Forbes, is wooded on the left bank, the woods at Castleforbes demesne. It is a pleasant interlude on the treeless banks and there we camped, gazing over the dark night-waters from behind our blazing campfire, while I relished the last pipe of the day, drawing long, slow pulls as I meditated on the sombre picture of the night.

At the lock of Termonbarry we met a barge of the Grand Canal Co hieing to Athlone with a cargo of turf. This was one of the only two locks that we entered in an orthodox manner. It was a large lock and we followed in behind the barge, holding the canoe snug against the wall by the hitching-ring while the water bubbled around us. I fell a-talking to the barge skipper, a tall, raw-boned man in the late thirties. He was not so surprised to see us as were the folk of the Inny and Lough Derravaragh, for canoes were common enough on the Shannon. For this we were grateful. After the first pleasant glow of being taken for a genuine *voyageur* and a dashing fellow, one is inclined to prefer being left alone and to avoid the repetitious questions.

The skipper decently offered us a tow and we assented readily. So we left the lock with *Minny* forlornly following at the end of her painter behind the chugging barge. Down in the tiny galley it was very snug and warm. We were treated to steaming mugs of tea and enormous slices of bread and jam. A clean tablecloth, a great square of brown paper, was laid on the table in our honour. Later, from a hidden closet a jeroboam of porter was secretively drawn and we whiled the jocund hours away in song, story and clatter. It is a very pleasant way of stealing a few miles from your journey, but, I confess, when I went on deck for a breath of fresh air, I found it hard to look *Minny* in the face as she wallowed helplessly like a sea cow in our wake. I felt we were not being honourable by her and promised her a rousing run on Lough Ree in rough weather to make amends. And sure enough she got it, and more than I bargained for.

Benny followed me up on deck and we sat there gazing over the banks that fled past at an accusing rate. 'You know,' he said, 'these fellows have been very decent to us.'

'They have that,' I answered. 'True Irish hospitality.'

'Well, do you think that's enough?' he asked.

'Enough? Good heavens man, what more do you want them to do?'

'Oh, you dolt. I don't mean them. I mean us. We ought to do something for them.'

'Yes, of course, we certainly should show our gratitude. Still, it is difficult to know what to do. If we offered them money they would throw us overboard.'

'I thought of that. But there is something else we could offer them.'

I stared at him for a minute, thinking of our poor fare and then his hint dawned upon me.

'Oh Lord, do you think…?'

'Well, we've nothing else.'

And so we made the greatest sacrifice we were capable of. Buried below all our potatoes and vegetables, our bread and our butter, and the conglomerated eatables in the large provision bag, was our secret hoard – a large tin of peaches. It sounds nothing now, but in that austere year, it was probably the only tin of its kind in the country. An exceptionally large tin, it had come from a hoard two years old and we had vowed to keep it for the most special of occasions, and to have a ceremonial opening with fitting music and speeches. In addition it was only to be opened on an uninhabited island on Lough Ree or Lough Derg, where there would be no danger of an uninvited guest showing up, so that we might gorge ourselves in solitude. We would take it out and brush it and fondle it now and again, and carefully restow it, so that it became a cant, in moments of anxiety on the river: 'Never mind the canoe, take care of the peaches.'

And this Lucullian dish was now to be handed over to the devices of three hungry bargemen. Well, we did it, and I never felt more a Christian than when we entered the galley, presenting our offering like a sacrifice and would not hear their courteous and genuine demurs. I believe they would have towed us to Limerick and back again to Carrick just out of gratitude.

We waited impatiently for Termonbarry, with its lock to Lough Ree. The men informed us that it was a dangerous lake, but as we had heard this about so many lakes we paid little heed. Yet we felt that they knew their business and were not spinning travellers' tales when they told us that very often the lake was impossible to the barges and that they had to run for shelter in rough weather to the sequestered little bays by the shore.

Indeed, at Termonbarry the great weir looked a formidable barrier and its roar indicated, more than words, the volume of water that spilled over it and the pace of the flow. The lock-keeper, in portentous tones, related a fatal boating accident of the previous year when a raw-boat was taken by the current and dragged over the lip of the weir, all five occupants being drowned. A grim heralding to the big lake.

But Ree looked peaceful when we entered it and once more took to the canoe, bidding fair weather and thanks to our generous hosts on the barge. She rapidly drew away and was lost to sight on the maze of the lake, her distant growling coming back to us across the still waters.

It was a very beautiful lake this peaceful summer evening and of a grandeur that we had not imagined, we who had thought Owel and Derravaragh sizeable enough. Lough Ree was aptly named the 'Lake of the King' and named, I hope, after its own regality, rather than after some forgotten kingling. Not very wide near the upper end, it stretched away beyond sight, widening all the time until, in the centre, it was about six miles across. But it was islanded, wooded, and here and there sheltered by low hills. The setting sun blazed like a stupendous jewel in the corona of the lake, burnishing its calm waters to a dazzling glow of reflection, except where, here and there, an island broke the brightness with a sombre shadow. The full peace of evening lay over it in a golden glory.

White markers showed the navigation channel to barges and large craft, as of old to the Shannon steamers, now gathered to the past, for passenger traffic on the Shannon and on its lakes is but a memory. We paid little heed to the markers, our minute craft permitting us to wander where we pleased, at any rate on calm water.

Filled with this bliss of lake travel at its best, we passed leisurely by Ferrinch, Goat, Inchenagh and Clawinch islands, deliberately dawdling to take in the prospect of the lake in full summer dress, with its innumerable shades of green, until we came to the large island of Inchcleraun, again with its ruins of seven churches, six of them being enclosed in the ruins of an old stone cashel. The original monastic establishment was founded by St Diarmuid, teacher of the famous St Ciarán, who founded Clonmacnoise. Here we came ashore.

Straight away we walked into a shepherd, a tall, large-limbed man, with unkempt hair and beard, wearing a very ragged suit, through which his dignity irradiated unlessened.

'Have ye any tobacco on ye, good men? and a fine day to ye,' was the greeting he gave us, a little unconventional, but warm and intimate. I was indeed sorry I had none and my friend did not smoke. Probably he cursed Lough Ree for sending him such useless strangers, for these war years were particularly hard on the people of the islands, who found it extremely difficult to obtain tobacco, cigarettes, tea and other things of this nature that once had been thought to be necessities. For the islanders, it was rendered doubly hard owing to the scarcity of paraffin for their boats, so that they found it difficult even to reach the mainland to get their rare supplies. He took my proffered cigarettes with ill grace, whipped the paper off them quickly, and not till the tobacco was thumbed greedily into his aged dudeen did he again break silence.

We wandered along the sheep track on the brow of the hill, the full beauty of the lake unfolding further to our eyes as we ascended the incline. And he talked of Inisclothran or Inchcleraun, his island, the island of Clothra. It was the island on which the Amazon, Maeve, warrior Queen of Connaught, spent her old age. There she lived in solitude and silence until well over the age of eighty years, wrapped in memories of war, bloodshed and rapine, heavy with the gloom of the hatred brought on by her quest for the Brown Bull of Culaigne, a quest that cost the flower of her knights and brought to death the brightest star of Irish pre-Christian chivalry, Setanta, the Hound of Cullan, that small, dark tempest of savage valour; and yet of a womanly gentleness. For there is no mythical hero of any legend quite like Cúchulain.

He is the epitome of the Celtic myth, the personification of their glories and dreams, and in him and in no other like him, not in Finn, not in Diarmuid, not in Oisín, not in Angus are the virtues and the savage war-lust of the Celt so vividly enshrined. In battle, said the Fileadh, schooled in subtle Druidic symbolism, he grew to twice his size, his eyes struck terror into his enemies, from his head gushed forth in a tall stream the uncontrollable blood of the war-frenzy, his arm was as of twenty men and in battle, over him shrieking the fearsome war-hymn, flew ever the dark raven, the Morrigan, Celtic demon of evil and death.

And Maeve, said the shepherd, talking quietly and unknowingly carrying his tradition of twenty centuries, bathed on the shore each morning, attended only by a solitary lady-in-waiting. From the mainland she was watched daily by Forbay, son of Conor mac Nessa, whose kingdom she had spoiled. He gauged the distance to her bathing-pool and assiduously practised with his sling, until he could hit an apple on a pole at the same distance. Then, one day, certain of his accuracy, he cast the stone that laid the old queen with her dead. He pointed out to us the place from which this missile is said to have been flung, and if he told aright, I take off my beret to the doughty Forbay, for it was a good mile away from where we stood. The ruins of the seven churches are so overgrown with brambles and nettles that they are well-nigh smothered under them.

So fond of solitude were we and so certain of finding it in this still region that, though we liked the place well, yet the fact of finding one house on it was sufficient to set us wandering again and we paused further down the lake in the enchanted evening. We padded slowly by a large *crannóg*, one of those mysterious habitations of a mysterious race of whom we know so little.

'... Slain so utterly

That even their ghosts are dead.'

What terrors and fearsome hunters did they flee to build such secluded and dangerous fortresses, when all around were islands for the asking?

We saw on the western bank a long line of woodland and thither bent our course. It was a most happy chance that brought us here, for it turned out to be the finest camping spot we had ever made. Nor ever afterwards have I met its like. Above the long, sandy shore was a carpet of soft, thick grass, sprinkled with moss-grown stones and this riparian strip ran for thirty yards or so in a gentle incline into the wood. Here, some hundred yards within, we found a little glade, sheltered on all sides by the encircling oak, smooth as a golfing green and ablaze with daisies. In this secret place we set up camp, breaking the silence almost in awe. We christened it 'the fairy glade' without ado, and indeed, had I seen a troop of the 'Little People' 'dancing to unearthly measure,' I should have stolen away again without surprise.

Before the sun had breasted the mighty crests of the oaks we were awakened by a very rain of birdsong that would have charmed the heart of Berlioz himself, who liked his choirs big. Blackbirds, thrushes, woodpigeon, finches, linnets, creepers, tits and heaven knows how many other species were singing their hearts out to the rising sun. On looking out through the tent-flaps I saw a rabbit a few yards away gorging himself on fresh, dew-washed clover. Scattered pairs of mallard whirred overhead to the shore. Everybody who was anybody in fur-and-feather-land was at breakfast. I took the hint and filled the pot from the lake.

Three days we remained in that bewitched spot and might be there yet had not our provisions given out. The days were idyllic. The sun shone brilliantly and we took our diversions as a gourmet might sample his wines, not for any need of the thing but to heighten the zest. One of us would go fishing in the canoe. Sometimes I took her out just so I could smoke at ease, stretched out on a pile of blankets, or anchor near the shore to read a book. The sun is always warmer near water, but you must keep the breeze out and a canoe is admirably designed to do just this. Or a bit of exploration in the big wood, with the bow for company, might bring one into sight of a sleepy pheasant dozing on a low branch. I have heard that Reynard has a subtle and curious way of catching his pheasant. He finds such a one, perched not far above the ground and after sitting staring at the bird for awhile until he has her attention well drawn to himself, he rises and walks slowly beneath her. She follows his course anxiously, until the sly dog rapidly increases his speed to a sharp trot, whereon the top-heavy bird is attacked by a dizziness and flutters helplessly to the ground. And dinner is served.

Once, too, coming back along the shore after a trek in the woods, I beheld a large jack-hare bouncing towards me. He stopped short on seeing me and I sped an arrow at him that pigged into the earth an inch from his nose. His amazement was so complete, as he sat bolt upright on his haunches without a trace of fear and stared at me, that I burst out laughing. He then bolted into the wood and escaped.

But I think that it was at night that we caught the deeper mystery of the place. The log fire threw a flickering in front of the tent, but beyond were impenetrable shadows and between the gusts that soughed in the trees could be heard the night noises, croakings and scamperings, growls or perhaps a shrill squeal as a rabbit fell to the marauding stoat. Overhead the woodcock passed with a shrill note. In the distance the very spirit of the eerie echoed in the hoot of an owl.

Here you could stretch on your back and look up to the ring of star-pointed sky, letting the mind wander at will, as it soared amongst the worlds, tying up, as it were, a dozen different philosophies into a bag in a vain effort to see the scheme of things as a coherent whole. And then, in weariness, giving up this question that we shall never answer on earth and spilling the bag again to the four winds. Indeed, it is at such a time that the walls of the flesh are most apprehended and that we realise how unutterable are the very depths of thought, as Patmore has it:

Views of the unveiled heavens alone
Forth bring
Prophets who cannot sing,
Praise that in chiming numbers
Will not run;
At least from David unto Dante none,
And none since him...

On Sunday, the fourth day of our sojourn in the Elysian fields, the gods evicted us. We ran out of the two most important essentials of a canoe trip: weather and food. The weather we could do nothing about, and as for food, we were almost completely destitute of it, and Athlone was the nearest point at which we could replenish our store. On Sunday evening, therefore, willy-nilly we had to set out in very rough weather for the latter town. It was hard going. The waves were boisterous, the wind roared across the open lake, the rain blew in squalls. Indeed, it was too bad to make Athlone and coming on Rinndun point we beheld the wide, open belly of the lake ridged with vicious white-caps. We were forced to pull in near the old castle, and as it was now getting dark we decided to set up camp near the open shore, a stone's throw from the famous old fort.

In the driving rain we took stock of our tiny store of victuals and found that they amounted to a little sugar, about half a loaf of bread and plenty of tea. We were very cold and hungry. We made our way to the dark, forbidding fortress and beheld smoke coming from among the ruins. In the old, inner courtyard, surrounded by massive walls, was a little cottage leaning against the angle of two walls. An old woman bade us welcome and on hearing our plight she gave us half a loaf of homemade bread, three eggs, a small bottle of milk and a handful of potatoes. She apologised for not having more to spare and my heart went out to her for her generosity. Such, indeed, is the hospitality we vaunt so much; and rightly, too, for it is a living thing, and often, as in this case, not given out of a plenty but out of a slender hoard. To her we made a gift of our spare tin of tea, for the poor creature had almost none. She would take no money either, but the tea was gratefully accepted, as it was the scarcest article in the district.

And so we rationed ourselves to a half loaf and an egg each, eating the bread dry. We kept the greater part of the food for breakfast, for we had a long, hard pull ahead. The night was wild and wet. It seemed the flimsy tent must surely be lifted out of the ground and flung across to the eastern shores, to Goldsmith's country and the remains of Auburn. Some of the guys were torn up by the wind and entailed a doleful labour, in the blackness and the rain, driving them home again. A small bank, on which grew a clump of thorn-trees, saved us from the full force of the wind. We heard the storm rage through the whole night around the ancient castle, once the powerful stronghold of the O'Connors, who regarded Lough Ree as their special territory.

Next morning we ate the last of the foodstuffs and set out for Athlone, about nine miles as the crow flies, but nearer twelve by canoe, in the weather we were having. We stayed in the centre of the lake most of the time, not trusting the shore for fear of shallows and rocks which were not visible in the muddy, disturbed water. Once we were driven aground on shingle in a cluster of tiny islands, the Cribbys, but found our way again without damage. The canoe was drenched from prow to stern as the waves pounded her. Before each squall of rain the wind blew with tremendous force and when the rain squall came, it was almost horizontal, blinding us and numbing the hands. One great gust blew the paddle out of my companion's hands and by good luck I pulled it down with my own paddle as it sailed past. We were very lucky here, as we should have had the paddles loosely strung to the boat to cover such an eventuality: it was difficult enough manoeuvring the canoe with two paddles, but with one, or even with single blades, it would have been an almost impossible task.

We left Rinndun at 10 a.m. and it was 5 p.m. when we drew ashore in sight of Athlone. We were pretty well spent, famished with hunger and wet through to the bone. The canoe had shipped a lot of water too, so that the first thing we did on landing was to light a large fire to dry our clothes, blankets and bags. Then, shivering, we reached the town and gorged ourselves on food. At such a time even the most hardened enthusiast would swap you his tent and boat for a meal and a fire.

When we reached the huge weir of Athlone we carried the canoe to the lower reach and some miles down set up camp on a long bald island in the river, which was here very wide. Having eaten again, for the sheer love of it and not from hunger, we turned in, crapulous but happy. Outside a persistent drizzle blotted the landscape with a veil of dismal grey.

We filled the provision bag to overflowing the following day, cramming it with luxuries that we normally would never think of buying. Biscuits, sweet cake, tinned salmon, Irish Gruyère, cooked ham, all went to stock the larder. For such is the effect of a day's hard rations that one takes every imaginable precaution against a recurrence.

For three more days we sat at the tent mouth gazing disconsolately out at grey banks, grey water, grey grey clouds, grey rain, making our memory of the 'Fairy Glade' even more like a dream. Everything outside the tent was soaking wet and we had decided, very reluctantly, to forego the rest of our planned trip owing to the general wretchedness of conditions. This was a very sore point with us who had so looked forward to Lough Derg, which was said to be an even more beautiful lake than Ree. But to have set out in such continuous rain and general drabness would have been utter misery.

So we lay in the tent for hours on end, reading and writing and fooling with a mouthorgan which neither of us could play properly. Once, after gazing long through the rain at the river, boredom so overcame us that, in a sort of violent rebellion against it, we stripped naked, ran at-full speed across the soaking grass, and plunged into the Shannon where we disported with great hilarity and on emerging, undertook a vigorous wrestling match while we rolled, alternately bellowing and roaring with laughter, through the long, steaming grasses. It is an odd thing how much weather affects one. It is not so bad in the city where there are so many diversions to be had indoor that the weather really is but a topic for conversation. I remember particularly two old soaks who spent most of their day in a public house and were forever growling and complaining about the weather.

'Did ye ever see anything like it, Mick? It's been raining now since Thursday without a stop.'

'Goddambut, Jack, it's the worst weather we've had since '29 and that's the truth I'm telling you.'

'Sure there's no chance of taking in the harvest at all if this continues and I wouldn't mind betting we'll have another famine on our hands.'

'Dreadful, dreadful. Ah, sure the world's changing for the worst every year. I remember when I was a nippereen...'

And so on. Yet it is doubtful if either of them was ever long enough outside a pub to get his ears wet.

But if there is one time when the weather is a genuine concern for every hour of the day and night, it is when one is camping. For we became as weather conscious on that island on the Shannon as the old man and woman that one sees in those ingenious little boxes that fortell rain or fair weather. But I had nearly forgotten. Providence, in a fit of pity, sent us one interest that almost compensated for the monotony of the rain. And this was the Almost Human Hare of Hare Island, the name of our camping ground. We saw him for the first time one day as we sat at our accustomed post, the door of the tent. We were full to repletion after a large meal, eating having now become the principal business of the day.

He hopped into view only a few yards away and sitting on his haunches stared in wonderment at the tent. Apparently he had lived alone on the island up to this and was feeling lonely. We stared back at him for a while and then Benny, still thinking of his belly, whispered, 'Get the bow.'

I drew it out and took a shot at him from within the awkward cover of the tent. Of course I missed, though narrowly enough and the hare took to his heels. We both ran out, I retrieving the arrow on the way. We chased him all over the island, sending arrows after him every time he stopped. Eventually he led us to a little enclosed field in the centre of the island, which was on rising ground and capped with a lone tree.

But a thick hedge surrounded the field and here he lay low, so that we lost him. We rambled back to the camp in good spirits, ignoring the rain which fell unceasingly. It was good to have some excuse to get out in it.

Half an hour later he appeared again, sat just long enough for us to get a shot at him and then bolted in short dashes ahead of us, giving us plenty of opportunities to demonstrate our inexpert prowess with the six-foot bow. When he had had enough of it he went to earth again in his little field.

First thing in the morning on opening the tent-flaps we beheld him contentedly chewing but a few yards away, patiently awaiting his playmates. Several times before dinner he hopped up again. Never was hare more sure of himself or showed such a contempt for his hunters. We began to hate him in our hearts for the way he showed us up, until there was a marked reluctance for either of us to take the bow and we became unctuously polite in offering each other first shot, the Almost Human Hare looking on with interest.

Eventually we pretended not to notice him, with a most carefully studied technique of turning our backs on him when he showed up. At this he became alarmed and hopped almost to under our noses, quite obviously asking 'What, are you not going to play today?' We detested the sight of him now and if he had come within reach of our bare hands, as he almost did, we would have strangled him without mercy.

As the next day was a little less wet, we took the opportunity to paddle down to see the ruins of Clonmacnoise. The river here was of a great width and when the wind rose it raised quite a popple. But the surrounding countryside was bare as a table and quite uninteresting. Huge meadows stretched on either hand, a solitary willow bending disconsolately over the bank at rare intervals. A lone farmhouse showed occasionally in the distance, surrounded by its wind-break of trees, for the wind blew over this naked plain without let or hindrance, curving the tall grasses and setting all the reeds a-shiver. Large herds of cattle grazing on either side of the river all along our journey were the principal sign of life in this silent land. It was just such a land as Joseph Campbell wrote of,

The silence of unlaboured fields
Lies like a judgement on the air:
A human voice is never heard:
The sighing grass is everywhere –
The sighing grass, the shadowed sky,
The cattle crying wearily!

Clonmacnoise loomed up around a bend of the river, a long line of buildings under a lowering sky. The walls of the ruins still stand in fair repair, the roofs having fallen long since. It too had its seven churches. The round towers show remarkable preservation, one of them still showing its pointed roof without a scar. The buildings extend for a considerable distance and in its glory Clonmacnoise is said to have housed two thousand students and was one of the greatest schools of Western Europe. Saint Ciarán founded it in 550 AD, he having studied under Saint Diarmuid on Inisclothran, the island already referred to in Lough Ree. It is said that Ciarán left his hermitage on a wooded island in a beautiful lake, maybe Lough Cé, and came here to settle in this bare windswept place that no natural loveliness might divert his mind from true contemplation and study.

The ruins of the seven churches of Clonmacnoise bring to mind the seven churches of Glendalough and many other places, which suggests that this number may have had a supernatural significance to the ancient Irish. Charlemagne sent a gift of money to Clonmacnoise in the ninth century, at the behest of Alcuin, when the school was at its greatest fame. The large cross of King Flann was erected over that prince's grave in the tenth century and stands today in an almost perfect state of preservation. So much so that the sculptured panels can be made out with ease; these, as in many Celtic crosses, show scenes from the Passion of Christ on the obverse side and from the Second Coming on the reverse – the Victim in his misery and the Judge in his omnipotence.

North of the plundered shrines, in a quiet field stand the remains of the Nun's Church, built by Devorgilla, wife of O'Rourke, Prince of Breffni, in the second part of the twelfth century. She was the unfortunate woman who was the direct cause of the coming to Ireland of the Normans who, invited to a battle, stayed for seven hundred and fifty years and who changed the history, the language, the conditions and almost the religion of the people. Devorgilla also gave a large grant to Mellifont, where she died. The large doorways still stand in her church at Clonmacnoise, fine examples of the Hiberno-Romanesque style with their dog-tooth arches and stone lacework.

But the history of Clonmacnoise and its repeated plunderings by Norsemen and no less savage natives, can be studied without my poor sketching of it. It is a place of proud associations for an Irishman and in these days of the rise of a new barbarism it would be a splendid thing to see this ancient cradle of culture rise from its ashes like a phoenix.

Coming home from Clonmacnoise and thinking of the weary miles against the current, we hit on the idea of a sail. So we lashed a paddle upright on the front of the cockpit and to it laced a strong triangular cycling-cape, one end playing free with the 'sheet' held by Benny; for laziness is as much the mother of invention as ever necessity is. With this jury-rig we travelled along in great style. We had neither lee-boards nor keel, but a paddle stretched out behind acted as both keel and rudder. It proved a very welcome relaxation from paddling against the current, though we were limited to catching the wind from dead astern or on the quarter. As the wind was strong and the river very broad, our speed was greater than when we came downriver with the current, using paddles.

The Almost Human Hare was sitting dejectedly in front of the tent when we arrived. We ignored him and set about dinner, while he nibbled his grass from a little distance, sitting up occasionally on his hind legs to see how things were getting on.

We determined to spend the last few days on Lough Ree as the weather had improved. On the way back to Athlone, out of a caprice, we started to 'collect' swans. There was a great number of these birds on the river and they seemed shyer than on the smaller rivers, for, on approaching them, they invariably took to flight, except on broad stretches, where they sidled by along the opposite bank. Now we headed for each group we met, not letting them pass, so that they had perforce to turn back upriver. We kept this up until we neared Athlone and had a prodigious number of the birds majestically sweeping the river before us. To a distant observer it might seem that Mananaan himself were arriving from Tír na nÓg in his magic boat.

As we drew in sight of the great weir, dozens of other swans coming downriver joined the flock. There must have been at least a hundred birds gathered together and we were growing a little apprehensive of what might happen should one of the cocks take it into his head to attack; whereupon we stopped paddling and drew into the bank. A few of the rearguard turned and commenced to swim downriver. Then, as they neared us they took to the air and were followed by others, until the greater number of the flock was rising and passing overhead. And what a whirr they made, what a splashing as they rose and what a breeze fanned us as they passed low overhead in a snow-

Pre-trip inspection.

On the Liffey, near Chapelizod.

Two views of the weir at Islandbridge taken in February 1941.

Benny at the fifth weir on the Liffey, May 1941.

Canoeing on the Liffey past rural pastures.

Royal Canal,
Enfield, June
1940.

Archery practice
near Maynooth on
the canal bank,
June 1940.

Further archery practice
on the banks of the
Royal Canal.

Lough Sheelin. 'Sheelin was not rough, but a strong wind
blew across, lifting little rollers that ran rapidly towards the
north-east shore.'

'The Tentmaker'. Below Carrick-on-Shannon on the first day out, May 1942.

'Fuel problem. What fuel problem?' The frying dell, Lough Ree, May 1942. The cook with his paraphernalia about to ruin dinner.

On Lough Ree,
May 1942.

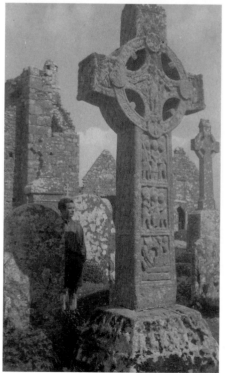

The Cross of
King Flann,
Clonmacnoise,
May 1942.

The Shannon.

On the Blackwater.

On the banks of the Blackwater, with Lismore Castle in the background.

Casting a weather-eye from the safety of the tent.

On the shore of Lough Oughter.

Killykeen Lodge, Lough Oughter.

Left Mending the broken wing of a tern, some 'sportsman' brought down with a shotgun. July 1948.

Below On Lough Oughter.

Lough Oughter Castle.

The farmer (displaying my gun and rabbit), a scoutmaster we met and Benny. Eonish Island on Lough Oughter, July 1948.

Left Cooking coot or 'old boot', as Benny termed it. 'I believe I could be there yet, patiently basting and blunting the fork on it...'

Below Taking a break from hunting and canoeing.

Right Benny illuminating the camp totem pole; one way of killing time.

Below Benny coming in to shore.

Above and below: Tent and canoe on the shores of Lough Corrib.

On Lough Corrib.

white cloud.

On Saturday evening we chose a heavily wooded island, about four miles from Athlone, to spend the last days of the trip. The weather was rather sunny, but sudden squalls of wind still heralded the cold showers and damped our desires to run to the mainland to see the country of Goldsmith. On such minutiae often hangs what we had considered an inflexible resolve. I travelled alone to Mass on Sunday morning, my companion being confined to his blankets with a dose of colic. In the early morning, wandering through the deserted streets of Athlone, I seemed to be the only person astir, for it is certain that we Irish are great sluggards on a Sunday. Until the circus came.

I stood on the path, watching the clowns cycling through the empty streets, the caravans and cages trundling by without their wonted horde of yelling small boys. Indeed, it was a dismal sight and till then I had never thought how glamour is a thing that we ourselves, as onlookers, go so much to make. Hardly a person in the town beside myself saw the cavalcade rumbling over the dusty streets. It looked just like any other business concern. When I entered a shop to buy tobacco, the woman said to me, 'Ye are early in town today,' and I mused on whether I should feel complimented. I had not thought our canoeing dress to be all that conspicuous.

In the afternoon I took the canoe out on the lake and foolishly, neglected to take some equipment as ballast. It was a lesson to me, for when I was a mile or two south of our island a strong wind arose and *Minny* was blown about like a cork. Only by heading straight into the wind, which, luckily for me, blew from the north-east, could I make any progress, slow though it was. The slightest deviation out of the wind exposed her prow, which would be blown aside like a feather, leaving the possibility of capsizing imminent. It took me quite a long time to make shore and I was more bothered than helped by shouted directions from my almost marooned companion; indeed, only by a series of rapid shufflings from stern to prow and back again did I manage to control the boat at all. A salutary lesson and one I did not need a second time.

In the evening we made Athlone together to see the circus. What a difference to the phantom caravan that had stolen through the town in the early morning. The noise, the lights, the glitter, the crowds, the band, the now wide-awake clowns and the snarling lions – these things we enjoyed with a zest that came from the contrast to our quietude and peace on the lonely waters.

But getting home brought back our quietude with a vengeance. As the circus went on until midnight, it was 1 a.m. when we set off up the river. There was not a star in the sky, nor a moon; as we left the last flickering lights of Athlone behind we paddled in a silence that could almost be felt and in a Stygian blackness. We were obliged to travel at a snail's pace and it took us two hours to find the dark island against the lighter darkness of the lake. Everything was as still as the grave, we did not hear even a night bird. This was the only night travel we made on this trip and it did not encourage another, though I dare say on a moonlit night it could have been very pleasant.

When we arrived we built the fire. This seemed to be the signal for the night noises to start. From the wood behind us came a succession of grunts, snarls, coughs, shrieks and timorous birdcalls. We looked at each other, startled, as the din continued.

We spoke in whispers, Benny hazarding a guess that a den of otters, badgers or both had been aroused. The occasional loud snapping of a twig or rustling of undergrowth, seemed to confirm at least that some sizeable animals were abroad. Taking counsel, still in whispers, we quietly loaded each an armful of heavy stones and at an agreed signal, opened up a fusillade fanwise into the encircling wood. We kept it up non-stop until our ammunition was spent and then began again. I am sure that the alarum was audible over that still, nocturnal lake for a great distance and many frightened bird calls showed that the missiles were disturbing their roosting. We ceased suddenly and silence flowed back over the island like a wave. There was no further sound for the night from the startled denizens of the wood.

The nights had grown cold and we thought of an excellent idea to heat the tent. From the huge camp fire we rolled a half-dozen large, red-hot stones into the foot of the tent and let down the flaps. In half-an-hour the place was like a steam-heated American drawing room and what was better, we rolled tightly up in the canoe bags, placed our encased feet on the 'hot-jars' and slept like infants. The hot stones will not burn heavy canvas and their heat lasts the whole night through.

We spent our last day trolling for perch. Lough Ree has a name for large trout, but again, we had brought no rod. I saw a fine specimen, three-and-a-half pounds weight in a shop in Athlone that had been caught the previous day at the northern end of the lake. The lady who had it on show in the shop was as proud of it as was her husband who had caught it. I hope they did not let it go stale through keeping it on show for admirers.

As we left, homeward-bound, with *Minny* tucked into her bags and lying ingloriously amongst the drab mundane baggage of the van, we passed over the fine railway bridge that here spans the Shannon and beheld the proud river stretching in a widening curve to where Lough Ree ends. To the south the Shannon spills in a wide cascade over the great weir and thence takes its leisurely way to Lough Derg.

We felt that the weather had cheated us of this lake and already fell to making plans for its exploration.

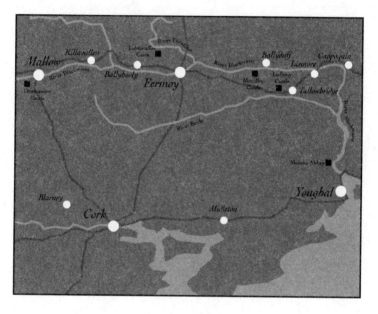

The Blackwater

THE BLACKWATER

If we liken rivers to women, then the Cork Blackwater is a tomboy – young, boisterous and beautiful. For it is a river with qualities all its own. It is virginal in freshness and beauty, it is fickle and changeable and in its short span one can sense the growth from gay irresponsibility and insouciance to maturity and a grave care. There is no other Irish river quite like it.

I remember Benny, who had cycled down to Mallow, asking the railway guard if he had a boat in the van. The man was amused at the question, thinking it a good joke; but when we hauled the bags out and told him that they contained our conveyance for an exploration of the Blackwater, he looked incredulous.

The source of the river is about thirty miles north-west of Mallow, but as it is very low in the upper reaches in dry weather, Mallow is the best point for a start and the most convenient rail centre. The river is but a few hundred yards walk from the station.

We struck abominable weather which lasted most of the trip. On any other waters we would have been greatly bored and would have probably concentrated on eating – a good way of forgetting your worries. But even in bad weather, it is a captivating river and in clear, sunbright days it must be an oasis of contentment. No Irish canoeist should forego it.

We pitched camp very late in the evening. It rained all night. It rained all the next day, too, heavy, vertical rods of rain that drenched everything and whose one redeeming feature to us was that they raised the level of the river and gave it a rapid flow. The most unsightly railway bridge I ever remember seeing spanned the river in front of the tent, adding to the bleakness of the prospect. Certainly it was a most unpropitious commencement to a tour. Out of sheer boredom we built the canoe in the rain and pushed off in the evening of the second day.

In the first hundred yards we bumped over small, bubbling shallows. We were to discover that the river was measled with them; they appeared every ten minutes for the first mile. The canoe had to be ferried over very broken water below the town bridge, where we were threatened by an alarmed swan, who made desultry forays against us while we were engaged in this awkward proceeding. It provided some amusement to the loafers on the bridge; none to us.

The banks were lined with many trees, which here and there spread into quiet copses. Shallows popped up unceasingly, small, noisy beds of fast water through which we blundered our way hilariously, shouting directions and warnings to each other which neither of us heeded. It was exciting and raised our rain-jaded spirits to a pitch of laughing and banter and to roundelays on the smooth after-flows.

Our first camp was in a meadow where we pitched tent in the dark amongst long drenching grasses and weeds. The owner, a young farmer, came upon us while we were unearthing a meal, somewhat like dinner, out of a mess of tins and pots. He warned us that a bull of his had a relish for this field and so, in the wet night, we struck the tent and found a safer site on the balk of a beet field, safe behind the bull-wire, while our friend kept up incessant chatter on trite topics of weather, beet, bulls, campers and like inconsequences.

Early afloat, the rain was still earlier. One can get used even to continuous rain, and life, though at a low ebb, goes on. Only occasionally a rabid litanising of epithets on the climate would boil out of us. We chanted them alternately, in strophe and antistrophe, Rabelaisian fashion:

This is a fiendish climate,
A Beelzebubbian climate,
A heresiarchal, anathematized,
Pestiliferous, pockified,
Blueprinted, scrofulous,
Sub-human, mildewed,
Diluvial, maledictory
.... climate

Thus relieved we bore the rigours of the day. The river flowed at a good pace and we did little paddling. I was reminded by our lazy progress of a canoeist I once met on the Liffey. He was travelling downstream on a streamlined, highly varnished copy of a Canadian birchbark, while we were struggling upstream against a heavy current. In conversation he mentioned that he never undertook the labour of upriver travel, but believed in always drifting downstream with a minimum of effort. It sounded sensible, but when I asked him how he got his craft back, he answered, 'Oh, I send one of the lorrymen down to collect it.' At that we parted company, for we did not consider him a canoeist at all, but a sham, a magnate, a tycoon who used the river as he would his manufactory; as a minion and a helot, to bear his jaded buttocks restfully along on fine hot days from source to wherever the spoiled breast took surfeit. Picture a canoeist who had never toiled upstream. What knows he of canoeing who only drifting knows?

The tall beeches, sycamores, chestnuts and willows alternated with the more homely whitethorn and ash in a variety of shades of green. The many rises were evidence of the salmon in this well-stocked river. Coot and waterhen jerked amongst the twittering rushes and a crane lazily drifted downriver upon our approach. Sometimes a belt of meadows or tilled fields added a pastoral peace where the river flowed black and deep. The ubiquitous shallows would come again in series, when the riverbed dropped its level. Many ruins stood on the pleasant banks, ruins of churches, castles, abbeys, fortified houses. Along practically the whole river we met these symbols of war and religion, which have given it the soubriquet of 'The Irish Rhine'. We stopped often to potter about the mouldering walls and cracked windows, but they were too numerous and too local, for the most part to incite any quest for their history.

There is a great variety on the Blackwater. At evening we came on a secluded stretch, that, on one side, was sheltered by tall cliffs, dripping with moisture and marked with deep green rash of mosses. From their summit hung sad drooping bushes and in this still place the splash of a leaping salmon made a great noise. Benny, interested in fossils, dug in the cliff base from the canoe and alleged that the cliff was a mine of interest, but I was too remote to know or care if he was right, for the rain had ceased and I was content to dream and doze.

We stocked our larder at Killavullen, a hamlet which also dreamed and dozed by the side of Mother River. Half the little shop's supply of tinned food was taken to feed our gargantuan appetites. Query: what did campers do before America put tinned foods on the market? If they lived off the land they very probably grew as tired of venison, salmon and roast duck as we did of tinned beans.

Of course the blame for restricted diet was due entirely to our romantic approach to the wide open spaces and a bed beneath the starry sky. The six foot bow, which was a sturdy weapon, would certainly have meant fine dinners if there was a capable archer to use it. Our simple trolling line, with a few spinners, restricted us to coarse fish. Neither of us was a rod

man, another of our great regrets. But say we had come armed
to the teeth with a couple of shotguns and a pair of salmon and
trout rods, well indeed might we have fared gastronomically on
these well-stocked rivers. Still, it is questionable if we would
have had the same primitive pleasure of the hunt, even when it
remained but a hunt, with no filled game-bag at the end of it.
The occasional grazier that fell to the bow was more than a
meal; it was a trophy and a symbol, and seemed the only honest
way to bring home your dinner and still keep your pride. But I
confess I had great sorrow about the rod. I contented myself by
false reasoning that we might have spent the trip around a good
hole and neglected travel.

Meandering again, we shot our quota of rapids for the day.
Of this we never tired. They were bigger now and more by
good luck than good guidance we escaped injury. I was not at
all sure that collapsibles were made for this pastime. Certainly if
waters are deep the collapsible is safe as can be, but in small
bumpy shallows, where one small rock may tear your bottom
out, a sturdier craft would add to peace of mind. Still, the fabric
in the collapsible is extraordinarily tough and upon inspecting
Minny each night all she showed of her day's buffeting was an
occasional scraping of the paint, with no real damage to the
fabric.

We camped on a thickly wooded and densely thicketed
island that night and sat around the large deadwood fire
watching its flickering rays throw dull light upon the fast-
flowing river. Rapids chuckled above and below us. Tall trees
sheltered us on all sides. When the rain came we moved under
canvas, stretched on our bellies on top of our blankets and
gazed into the embers, which hissed and spluttered in the drops;
and we talked in low tones for hours, on the Celts, druids, fire-
worship, megaliths, matriarchy and things generic.

In the morning we pushed off after gazing for a long time

on the uncanny gyrations and lightning-like darts of a flock of swifts, that played around the island like a school of young aviators trying out a new type of jetplane. It seemed to be mostly play, little feeding being done and sometimes, one of these feathered meteors whizzed by our ears with inches to spare. This bird is said to attain a speed of 150 miles per hour and undoubtedly, looking at them on the wing, they surpass all other birds so greatly in both speed and manoeuvrability, that at times the eye can hardly follow them.

Downriver, we drew ashore to examine a tall, ivy-covered watchtower which, in good preservation, still held its solitary outlook from a thickly wooded hill. From the parapet a wonderful prospect extended below for many miles. The twisting river brightened here and there through the green crowns of trees and a series of little green hills rose unobtrusively by lush meadows and ploughed land on the right bank. Behind us were woods, falling in terraces of many hues to a distant plain. Small farmsteads dotted this truly pastoral scene, while a ruined castle or ivied keep, thrusting above the trees, marked the long dead vigilance of some petty warlords. All along the river these old keeps rose regularly in their picturesque surroundings to show how coveted was this rich land in the days when a man's possessions were measured by the strength of his strong right arm.

On a quiet stretch of river we were surprised to come upon flagpoles with bunting and pennants gaily splashed across the river and merrily blowing from the trees. A long greasy-pole stretched over the river and we knew that some village sports had been held. On looking at the map we found that we were near the village of Ballyhooley and decided to pay it a call. The village slept at the end of a long boreen which we followed from the river. Indeed it might have so slept for centuries for not a solitary person was to be seen in the main street. We expected it to be quiet, as it was Sunday, but certainly not in *rigor mortis*.

'I could do with a drink,' I said to Benny. 'Do you think I might get one today? After all, we are travellers and not your three-mile *bona fide* ones, either.'

'My ingenuous friend,' said he, helpfully, 'no hostelries or taverns are permitted to trade in intoxicating liquors in rural Ireland on a Sunday. That privilege is reserved for the "dhroots" of the cities. But here they are under the watchful eye of the local sergeant and all must be honest men.'

'Well,' I answered, 'if you mean to tell me that, in this village, just after having its annual gala, not one citizen is at this moment quenching his legitimate thirst illegitimately, like Captain Marryat's Hudusi, I "very much doubt the fact." Where's everybody, anyway?'

'Innocently sitting by their firesides, where they should be and not slobbering up the main street with their tongues indecently salivating in public for the want of drink.'

Here he showed the guilelessness of the abstainer and the consequent ignorance of the ways of the peasantry of this land. For to us 'the bottle' is what the drinking-hole is to parched animals in a forest. Indeed it is more, for few go to a pub merely to quench thirst. But we, more perhaps than other peoples, are a nation of talkers and beer is the oil that clacks the tongue. If any further proof of this little homily were needed, which I gave Benny in a few words, discreetly, kindly, and for the good of his soul, it was given when I marched over and knocked boldly on the doors of a public house, which, to all appearances, was as empty as the tomb. But after a lot of shuffling and whispering, not at all ghostlike, the door of the tomb opened an inch, into which I called the magic word, 'Travellers'. Whereupon it was thrown open and we with difficulty found our way to the bar through the packed innocents of the village. I enjoyed my drink, for I was truly thirsty. But I think the whole male population of the place was crammed inside and there was no comfort.

We eased ourselves quietly out of this thirsty village and once more between our beloved screen of trees, drifted at a soporific rate over the pale sunbeams that glided through the leafy arch. Deliberately we set a very slow pace, so as to space the short stretch of the Blackwater over our two weeks holiday. If we had hurried we could have been in Youghal in three days from starting. But we were learning wisdom slowly and each trip grew lazier and more perfect, so that the memory only of our first wild timetable trip was enough to make me wince. Thus, too, we took it easy at our camps. If we liked the spot we would spend two or even three days idling busily at unimportant chores. The deep pleasure I found in these comes back to me often in a mellow memory. Stretched out beside the fire, clad only in bathing shorts, soaking up the heat of both the sun and the fire, I took more pains and interest in refeathering an arrow, stitching a camera case or gluing a broken back-rest than ever a patient scribe took with his illumination of a manuscript.

These insignificant things would take on an altogether exaggerated importance. I have seen Benny, who was more painstaking than I, spend the whole livelong day, apart from breaks for meals, endeavouring, with a kit of tools, to repair the broken spring clip of a camera. And to give him credit he succeeded. Oh, the glory of idleness! We understood those negroes well that Mark Twain tells of, sitting all day on the burning banks of the Mississippi and keeping from lapsing into complete senility by 'jes' whittling'. But there are degrees of idleness and we baulked this. Or maybe the sun was not hot enough, for on really warm days I have enjoyed same whittlin' myself.

Fermoy looked a bright, cheerful town as we drew above its fine old bridge, For some reason that now I cannot remember, we lifted the canoe over the weir and paddled away as if there was no town there at all. It was an odd thing to do, especially with such a cheerful-looking and historical town. We, who drew ashore at almost every village on the route, bypassed this decent town with a nonchalance that, looking back, astonishes me. Certainly 'a boy's will is the wind's will' and not to be accounted for. Probably we had a full provision bag and had no interest in towns except as replenishment stores. Or, more probably, the beauty of the river country had eaten into us and every hour away from it was an hour lost of a very pleasant dream. But I'm sure that Fermoy bore up well under its great loss.

While I cannot recall a thing about Fermoy, I remember Ballyduff well because of the great contrast I saw there between placidity and exertion. Exertion was the enormous bull, which we heard long before we beheld him. As we came near, we saw this lively ox cantering up and down his field, bellowing loudly. He seemed in a pretty humour for, beholding us, he charged down to the river bank and bellowed worse than ever. He never stopped bellowing. We were quite scared, as there was no fence on the bank of his field and he seemed mad enough to dive in after us. But we passed by almost on top of the further bank, while the irate bull kept pace on his, giving us incredibly dirty looks, stamping, lashing his tail and roaring to heaven.

Placidity was a little further downriver. There, drunk in the sunshine, sprawled Ballyduff, in a Constable setting; old rustic bridge, (alas, the mill was lacking) white, dusty roadway, thatched cottages, dogs dozing and all sheltered by great high banks of trees. Passing quietly through the village, so as not to disturb it, we set out for a market garden a mile or two up the road, and coming circuitously, we again passed by the field of Exertion, who, beholding us passing by his gate, made a wilder charge than ever and bellowed with a prodigious bellow. As we fled up the road we heard him worrying the gate with his horns. Perhaps he was the guardian of the peace of the sun-meshed village.

Below Ballyduff the river gradually grows deeper and wider. This is a very lovely stretch. There is here the sense of being hundreds of miles away from cities, and this alone justified it to us. Indeed, in such an ancient, quiet beauty, it seems at times quite difficult to fathom why men have locked themselves up in these great, concrete husks that sap the vigour and the innocence of a man like an insidious disease. I believe if the cities could sap his humour they would make an end of him, but this is impossible and instead the monster warps it. Which, in a way is almost as bad.

We lazed on towards Lismore. Here we again tried sailing. It proved a humourous business, for we had neither keel, lee-boards, nor rudder. We lashed a spare strut to the front of the cockpit and as on the Shannon, tied our black triangular cycling-cape to it. In a series of drunken lurches from one side of the river to the other, we made a snail's pace. But the primary object was achieved: we had no paddling to do. And let the sail do what it might it could not carry us backward; the flow of the river saw to that. It was reminiscent of Lear's nonsense rhyme, 'The owl and the pussycat went to sea, In a beautiful pea-green boat…'. Appropriately enough, *Minny* was of a pea-green colour.

Rounding a bend in the river, or better, reeling round a bend in the river, we noticed a considerable widening and there was an ominous flow that one finds invariably above a weir: not rapid, but widespread, quickening and of great power. We whipped down the handkerchief of a sail and heaved slowly back on the paddles. We could hear the muffled roar of falling water quite near, but there were none of the usual signs of a weir. Indeed, straight ahead, the river appeared to end suddenly beneath a grove of great trees. We drew ashore onto the right bank to reconnoitre.

We found we were on a tiny, wooded island connected to

the right bank by a small bridge over a sluice, now closed. Walking to the further end we found that a strong stone pier had been constructed against the island bank and directly across from it, about eighteen feet away, was another. Through this gap the broad river tumbled with a loud roar, the fall being about four feet, but of great speed. Large pancakes of yellow foam bobbed about the edges of the permanent upsurge that spilled into white froth for many yards.

This was the famous salmon weir of Lismore. On the calm water beyond we saw a narrow high-prowed skiff moving towards us, oared by four brawny fishermen. Behind them, sheer from the river bank and appearing as if growing from the tall crowns of the trees, rose the broad towers and castellated battlements of Lismore Castle, a magnificent pile that added a medieval atmosphere to this sylvan scene. This fine castle, now a seat of the Duke of Devonshire, once belonged to Raleigh, who sold it to Richard Boyle, afterwards created Earl of Cork. The latter worthy shows how a fortune was made in those days, for he tells us himself, that upon landing in Dublin in 1588, 'All my wealth then was twenty-seven pounds three shillings in money, and two tokens which my mother had given me, viz., a diamond ring, which I have ever since and still do wear, and a bracelet of gold worth ten pounds; a taffety doublet cut with and upon taffety, a pair of black velvet breeches laced, a new Milan fustian suit laced and cut upon taffety, two cloaks, a competent linen and necessaries, with my rapier and dagger.' When he died he left a large estate to each of his children, of which he had altogether thirteen. Even before his time, Lismore was renowned as a seat of learning, boasting a cathedral and some twenty churches as long ago as the eighth century, and Alfred the Great is said to have been taught the use of the harp there.

But our problem was how to fetch our loaded craft below

the picturesque obstacle below us. We spoke to the fishermen, who had drawn close up to the weir-foot. They recommended carrying the canoe over the closed sluice. This, however, we were loath to do, firstly because of laziness, and secondly, because we wanted to shoot the weir. The men were not very sanguine of our chances and spoke of the danger of breaking the back of the canoe as she would travel over the hollow of the fall. I found a compromise in emptying the canoe of all our chattels and taking her over myself; thus, being very light, the risk was small. I fitted the spray-sheets and took my old place in the stern.

Paddling out to midstream, the canoe was quickly caught by the rapid and powerful current and carried silently towards the weir. As I came near I leaned well back and gave a few vicious paddle-thrusts. She leaped over the edge, plunged almost halfway under the upsurge, bounced up again like a cork and in a few seconds, dripping all over with spume-pools, shot at a tremendous rate over the rough to the smooth water beyond. The fishermen gave a little cheer, standing upright in their skiff, and enjoying the proceedings.

Later, having pitched camp in a nearby glade, we strolled over to the fishermen's hut for a yarn. They were quiet, brown-faced men, solid and like most of their sort, full of a serenity and imperturbability that seem a hallmark of their calling. We went out with them late in the night in their boat to see them dragging in their nets at the foot of the weir. They told us that the Duke had the right of netting the salmon on their way upriver for eight hours of the twenty-four. This privilege was bitterly resented by the amateurs, many of whom we had spoken to along our route. The Duke's salmon are shipped to the London market. But after toiling for an hour in the dark night, the men took but two fish, about sixteen pounds apiece.

The bailiff came upon us as we washed ourselves in the shallows of the river next morning under the tremendous walls of the castle, to satisfy himself that we were legitimate travellers and not poachers in disguise. He gave us a warning that proved useful regarding a dangerous curve in the river, below the next shallows. He too, painted lurid pictures of dangers in the tidal reaches, rocks, snags, mudbanks and the like. As was often the case, the warnings, though well meant, were exaggerated or inaccurate.

However, as we bounced over the shallows later in the evening, having, in the blithe wilfulness of youth, completely ignored Lismore town as we had Fermoy, we had reason to thank him for his first warning. For, beside a mudbank, there appeared the ugly snout of a submerged tree, its long bare boughs stretching far out under the surface. A little stream, in flood, that entered at this point, made a dangerous current and altogether it was an ugly piece of work. It could have done a lot of harm to *Minny*. But thanks to our friend, we were prepared for it and waded by on the shallow side.

Beyond that place it was plain sailing. As we neared Cappoquin, the flow of the river gradually decreased, the banks receded and the ample waters showed that we were coming into the tidal reaches. This was big-river canoeing, lazy, easy, safe travelling, but we missed the friendly proximity of the trees and the bucking of the little rapids that give a gaiety to river travel.

We drew ashore at Cappoquin for a meal. While eating, we debated on making a visit to Mount Melleray, which was but four miles away. Laziness again triumphed, I am sorry to say, and afterwards I regretted very much not visiting the famous Cistercian monastery and its silent monks. We must have been indeed creatures of impulse in those halcyon days, as careless and reckless as the rivers we loved.

Shortly after leaving Cappoquin, Benny developed cramps in his stomach. He blamed a bottle of sauce upon which he had feasted to an inordinate degree, in a dark little restaurant in the town. These cramps seemed to take all the spirit and strength out of him and he took to moaning and groaning, the while rubbing and massaging his abdominal muscles. As the aches grew worse he sandwiched some choice language between groans, not a bit complimentary to the good town of Cappoquin, its inns and its condiments. Strangely enough, I was not moved to sympathy by this strange way of expressing great anguish and I began laughing, which soon grew into one of those fits over which one loses control, so that I could only have laughed the louder had my poor shipmate expired under my unsympathetic eyes. There we were, two men in a boat, out on the broad river, one doubled in pain and uttering the most blood-curdling lamentations and moans, the other stretched out in a helpless laughter-fit. It must have been a puzzling scene to any bystander on the banks.

However, as I had to do the paddling for several miles, I began to suspect the genuineness of these convenient pains. It was tiring work, coaxing single-handed a loaded canoe on the sluggish river and when I told Benny I was beginning to feel very queer in the stomach myself, he began to improve rapidly; more so when I ceased paddling altogether and the canoe, amidst the two sets of groans, began to drift aimlessly on the river. We decided on a shore call and once the paddles were out of sight, we both showed a remarkable recovery.

We had landed on an island and it was soon obvious that we were intruders. The island had been completely taken over by rabbits. Never in all my life have I seen so many rabbits. They started up under our very feet and the burrow-pocked ground was dotted with twitching ears and disappearing scuts. When I went back for the bow I discovered to my disgust that I had but one arrow left and the flight was ragged and loose. However I passed half-an-hour fooling around the place taking random shots with the wretched arrow. I was treated to a display of indifference that hurt me. These rabbits must not have been hunted from year's end to year's end. Not hunted, that is, by man. But they had not escaped their relentless enemies of the fields, for among some brambles I heard a shrill squeaking and breaking through, something brown and furry ran across my foot. It was a stoat and when I lifted his young victim from out of the thorns, I saw that the wicked little brute had eaten through the haunches of the young grazier into the liver. The grazier was still alive, but paralysed in the rear legs. I put him out of his pain quickly.

There must have been quite a colony of stoats on the island, for, in the dusk, as we sat around the fire, we heard shrill squeals issue from various parts of the island. It was evident, as Benny put it, that the stoats were 'making hay'. Certainly they had come to a rich territory. Another little nature cameo I watched just before dark fell. On the riverbank I heard a bird singing, and while I looked for him among the branches of a young tree, I saw another vigilant brown hunter move in silent silken bounds down the fields to the river edge. He disappeared from my view for a few seconds. There was a sudden stop to the birdsong, a fluttering of branches, and silence. This killing must have been going on day and night and I wondered how the stoats on the island had crossed the river. Probably they had swam across, as being rodents, they would have no terror of water.

We spent two days on this quiet and secluded island and by then the rabbits would almost talk to us, so that neither of us had the heart to try shooting them. In the early morning, as we washed in the river, scores of swifts darted along the dark, swirling water, travelling soundlessly. In the afternoon, having nothing better to do, we stretched out by the log fire and sang songs. The power of association is very strange and very strong. When one is in a reverie, as I was then, the rise and fall of old, familiar melodies touches half-forgotten memories and quickens them to new life. I think music, more than any of the arts, has this haunting quality of timelessness that makes us one with the past and drenches the soul in a mist of beauty, 'This beauty that must pass.' One old song of Benny's, 'I fear no foe in shining armour' brought vividly before me a stretch of fast, rapid-strewn river, hemmed in on both banks with thick woods. Down this we drifted, three of us, the only time we allowed a third in the little craft. But she was slim and small and her dark head rested back against my knees as we glided to the haunting cadences of the melody, sung in unison.

Then as we ranted the rollicking sequences of the 'Jolly Friar', there came a memory of a bleary Christmas Eve, a crowded restaurant and an uproarious table of convivial spirits joining in the lilt of the chorus. The rest of that night was hazy with the fumes of Burgundy, no doubt as the Friar himself would have it. 'An Spalpín Fáineach', sung in Irish, painted the Liffey in high summer; low water, blazing sun and solitude. I could recall, with extraordinary clearness, the exact bend of the river and the large, ugly snag of log that marked it, where first I heard this lovely ballad chanted.

And so with other songs. I rambled down the lanes of memory and lived again some pleasant hours, called back effortlessly by the magic of song.

To me there is a fascination about rivers, that, instead of fading through familiarity, grows stronger with the years. One reason is the subtlety of their moods. The Blackwater was now, shall I say, in her early thirties, full-grown, spacious, ripe in knowledge, and with the gravity that becomes one who has outgrown the pranks of youth and has seen a share of life. Large dun mudbanks, revealed in their ugliness by the falling tide, stretched below the soft earthbanks, which gave evidence of their continually caving in. Old dead trees, slowly suffocating in the slime, thrust wild crooked arms above their mudgraves.

Alongside one bank we saw a small schooner, so that we knew we soon would come upon the sea.

We camped beside the ruins of Ballintrae Abbey, where is buried Raymond le Gros, who accompanied Strongbow to Ireland. It is a quiet, secluded spot, one admirably suited for contemplation, for, in the grey, sunless evening the tranquil melancholy of the river silences enter into the soul, hinting at strange undercurrents of thought, below the level of consciousness.

Out on the broad breast of the river, with the banks now distant on each hand, we paddled rhythmically and without pause, covering the miles at a good pace. Away ahead of us loomed up the long bridge of Youghal. It is of a great length, but is strictly utilitarian and has no pretensions to beauty. We had scarcely passed under the arches when the whole forward end of the canoe heaved up and dropped back onto the water with a heavy slough.

'What's that?' asked Benny, who had been looking astern when this happened.

'Might be a big salmon leaping,' I replied, hopefully.

'If they've salmon that size around here,' he said, 'they'd need to harpoon them instead of using flies.'

We coasted watchfully, warily eyeing the area near us. Suddenly a huge, grey, slimy back appeared a few feet away and a tall triangular fin disappeared in its wake.

'Salmon?' Benny's arched eyebrows evidenced wonderment and anxiety. 'Let's get out of here. But quickly.'

Before he had finished we were digging away at full speed for the shore, which seemed a vast distance away. As we bustled along, the grey back and dorsal fin appeared at intervals, now astern, now ahead, now on the quarter, often dangerously close. We now knew it to be a porpoise, and its idea of a playful evening, innocuous enough to steamboats, was anything but appreciated by us. Indeed the first rise had almost capsized us.

Benny wanted to have a shot at it with the arrow, but I was afraid of infuriating it, even if I should be lucky enough to hit it. The big fish followed us all the way to shore, where an interested crowd of onlookers followed the scene in amused safety. When we reached the shallows our hospitable porpoise continued gambolling and cavorting for a long time a little way out, and we had to skirt the headland in tricky narrows, before he lost the scent, or whatever it is that porpoises lose.

As we rounded the point of the headland we, for the first time, felt the rhythm of the mighty Atlantic. The sea was quite smooth, and to the eye showed no movement worthy of notice. Yet we felt the canoe slowly lifted on high, and with taut stomachs, felt her slowly rolled down again. One experiences the feeling of immense power with little evidence of effort. What this ocean must be like in a strong gale I was not anxious to discover.

The swell was more evident on the beach where the sea broke in curling rollers that rattled and snaked along the sands before they ran back into the suck of the recoil. The beach was crowded, it being a fine sunny day and we decided to show off. Unlucky moment! We rose on a big roller and paddled furiously with it so that we were flung ashore at a fast speed. To demonstrate to the uninitiated onlookers our expertness at this sort of thing, I back-paddled furiously as the roller petered out, thus leaving the canoe broadside, high and dry. Somehow I thought this looked more seaman-like than having her fore and aft, it smacked of warping onto a wharf. Next instant a following roller poured over us before we had time to step out of the craft, filling us with about a foot of water. We hopped out soaking, the urchins around yelling their delight.

When we had hauled *Minny* out of harm's way we discovered that all our blankets, food and clothes were wet through. We had to spread them on the beach to dry under the cynical eyes of those onlookers which we had expected to be glowing with admiration. Then, to draw even more unwanted attention to ourselves, an urchin of tender years picked up the bow that Benny had left carelessly unattended. The embryo Robin Hood let fly an arrow that whizzed within an inch of a recumbent fat man's nose and brought that worthy to sudden life. He jumped up, and seeing Benny holding the bow which the terrified lad had instantly dropped, the near-victim instantly declaimed against the stupidity and carelessness of overgrown schoolboys, and threatened to break our bow across his knee. He, though, showed no anxiety to carry his threat into execution. In my turn, I was treated to a philippic by my companion as being the cause of all our woes. I was feeling duly chastened, and murmuring something about exercise and fresh air, I set off for a perambulation on the beach.

Youghal is a fine old town and to us seemed a lively, bustling place compared to so many of the sleepy towns and villages through which we had passed. There appeared to be an Elizabethan freshness about it, though why this should be so I cannot say. Perhaps the bracing Atlantic air and the associations with Raleigh had something to do with it. His house, as everybody knows, is still there and should be there for a long time yet, as no one is allowed to enter it; which is an admirable method of preserving monuments, and much loved of the Board of Works, who stick unsightly iron railings around a ruin and put up a large bilingual notice warning everybody against violation; but they never print a solitary word about the history of the structure or its associations. In this house Raleigh is said to have entertained Edmund Spenser, who blew the first, fragrant puff of genuine Virginia under a famous yew tree on the lawn of the manor. Here, too, Raleigh is said to have planted the first potato and one wonders how the nation had managed to feed itself at all before this revolutionary innovation, or what forgotten and mysterious viand had till then accompanied the bacon and cabbage to table. Perhaps indeed, there was only the bacon. Did not Cromwell bring over the cabbage? If only we could discover an Englishman to have introduced the pig we might for ever hold our peace.

It is not Raleigh, however, but one Thomas Heriot, a mathematician, who first introduced the potato into England, having brought one back in his pocket from the new colonies, to cure rheumatism. Earlier, the tuber had been used in Southern Europe, no doubt being one of the first American exports. The potato has undergone a curious transformation since its first introduction to these islands about 1584. Then it was carefully nurtured only by the nobility and was supplied as a great delicacy to the Queen of James I's household at the price of 2/0 the pound. Later still, in the early part of the eighteenth century, it was looked down upon and Evelyn wrote, 'Plant potatoes in your worst ground.'

Gradually the fine properties of the potato were discovered and proclaimed. In our own country, as well as in others, the root became the main, indeed, almost the sole fare of the people. With what calamitous results we know too well.

This extremely pleasant trip concluded with an amusing incident. We rose at 6 a.m. and without our breakfast, that we might save time, we commenced to break camp and to take down the canoe. Either of these operations may take some time: together, it is a lengthy and harassing proceeding, and one never seems to be able to pack all the equipment compactly, although much less is involved than upon starting, as the foodstuffs are finished. It is rather like taking apart an alarmclock and finding lots of wheels left over upon reassembling. Despite our frantic efforts, we beheld the train puffing out as we secured, with apoplectic faces, the last strap. There being several hours to wait for another train, we left the bags in the station and sauntered through town in our military capes and berets.

For no other reason than that we felt in high spirits, we commenced talking in loud voices a macaronic jargon of German, Spanish, French and Latin phrases, especially when passing policemen, who stood and stared after us. We were highly amused at the effect, until we strolled back onto the crowded railway station, and beheld several gardaí lolling about. I was reminded of the swans we had collected on the Shannon.

A plain-clothes officer approached us and asked us courteously to come into the station master's office. Three lolling gardaí brought up the rear. Inside, I was given over to the plain-clothes man for interrogation (no doubt as being the more dangerous-looking of the pair) and the sergeant tackled Benny. I was cross-examined very minutely as to our origin and movements, and especially as to how we had come to drop in so casually on Youghal from the open sea. For it transpired that so we had first been observed, and the ubiquitousness of the guards in our travels through town had been no mere accident. We had been under close surveillance all the time, for at that time German submarines had endeavoured to push ashore in a few places, agents of their Secret Service. While I was desperately trying to prove our good faith to the highly suspicious minion of the law, I heard loud words bandied about in a corner of the room.

My trouble-loving shipmate was treating the sergeant to a tirade in Irish and the unfortunate man couldn't understand a word of it.

'Now listen here, young man, all I want is your name and address and none of your cheek or shouting.'

Benny (in Irish): 'I have told you several times. It is (in slow measured tones) Bernaird Uai Brádaig.' Then it was spelled letter by letter.

Guard: 'Wait now, wait now. B-E-R. What's after R ? U-A-I. Are you sure this is your right name? Why the hell can't you speak English?'

Benny in Irish: 'Irish is the official language of the country and you are an official. If you don't know the language that's your worry.'

Guard: 'I don't know what you're saying, young man, but I don't like the way you are saying it.'

In desperation the red-faced guard turned to the rest of the company. 'Does anybody here know Irish?' There was an uncomfortable silence and the station master, saying he had to look after the train, went out. After some mumbling and another vehement tirade in the official language by Benny, the sergeant and my interrogator went into a huddle in the corner, comparing notes in undertones. They were very suspicious of us and after a lot more questioning of me – for they now ignored Benny, who stared belligerently at them and put in an occasional barb of wit which, though not understood, was sensed – they let us go, with a bad grace, and no doubt felt they were risking the neutrality of the country by their generosity.

We caught the train with some minutes to spare and had a long laugh over the affair on the way home.

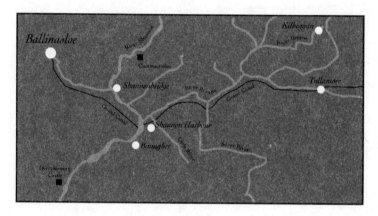

The Brosna

THE BROSNA

There are advantages and disadvantages in picking out a thin blue line on a map and saying, 'We start here,' without knowing the first thing about the stream. The advantage is the novelty and the feeling of being the first to navigate some tiny trickle of water, which may lead nowhere. The disadvantages are obvious, the worst being that there might be no water at all, if the summer is dry.

We had determined to finish the Shannon and to run Lough Derg, so we picked out the Brosna on our Ordnance map and set off for Tullamore in fine sunny weather. But as a canoe trip it proved a failure, through a mischance. As a camping holiday it turned out to be the *pièce de résistance*.

We commenced on the Tullamore River, a quiet pastoral little stream that meanders gently through the town, no one paying much attention to it; and then wanders aimlessly amongst the meadows, hillocks and copses of Irish Central Plain country. Here and there it got lost in a bog, but found its way out again. The weather was dry; a most fortunate dispensation: not warm except in occasional splashes of sunshine, but equable and dry. We had passed under the Grand Canal and had come but a few miles from Tullamore, when disaster struck. We had come on a diminutive weir about two feet high, over which the lazy Tullamore River tumbled in a half-hearted way. Deceived by this insouciance we forgot our usual caution, and instead of lifting *Minny* carefully over the obstacle, we each took prow and stern painter and heaved her casually onto the lower level. Fellow-canoeists take warning. Our fully-loaded craft pitched sideways in the wash and instantly shipped a large flow from the weir. I gave a great heave on the stern painter to lift her clear, when there was a horrible tearing noise as a foot or two of the covering fabric ripped off together with the metal stern strengthener. We instantly jumped into the river and with a tremendous effort hauled the now astonishingly heavy canoe onto the bank, taking care to spill as much water as possible out of her so as not to break her back.

The damage was bad. The rip had gone to within two inches of the waterline. It was clear she was beyond lake-travel, especially on Lough Derg. It looked like the end of the trip before we had begun. Everything was soaking. Luckily the sun was shining and we spread the blankets and clothing on the whins to dry. Benny again proved the good shipmate. Instead of wasting time and fraying tempers with useless recriminations, he satisfied himself with one long blue sentence of epithets and then shut up and busied himself with dinner.

I decided we would have to do with running repairs and limit our explorations to the Brosna, as even the stretch of the Shannon from Shannon Harbour to Lough Derg would be dangerous in such a condition; for the Shannon can raise a popple in a wind. So I stitched the fabric with a curved upholstery needle and strong linen thread from the repair-kit and over the stitching solutioned a large piece of single-ply repair fabric. It was a rough job, but it held for the trip, as no heavy water came into contact with it.

My camera too, had been immersed in the river and had to be thoroughly dried. But the shutters were slowly sealing with rust and only two or three wretched over-exposed pictures remained to remind us of this pleasant little journey. In the evening we came in the midst of a bog and as it was so still and quiet we pitched camp on a green patch beside the river. It proved to be a great haunt of snipe; they flew up with a whirr from under one's feet and circled high above our heads, their loud drumming echoing above the bleak bog. This drumming is done with the tail-feathers, but it sounds much more like the 'baa-ing' of a goat than a percussion instrument. Plover, too, flopped lazily on the wing, their plaintive 'Pee-wit, pee-wit' dripping like rain above our heads.

Here after dinner I developed acute diarrhoea and for this I blamed the river water, but as my companion did not suffer, it would seem to have been something else that caused it. It was extremely enervating and lasted most of the next day. This was the only time I ever suffered from this illness while camping, and though I was very curious to find the cause I was not successful. We invariably used lake or river water for meals and it is quite safe. But beware of small streams or rivers below towns, in these cases it is safer to forage for a well.

Next day I felt so miserable and my stomach was so upset, that I took a powerful emetic and expelled the offending germs from my system. I felt well instantly, like one switching on a light. I suppose this is the way with nature's child – no slow dragging illness or convalescence, but quick and painful sickness followed by rapid recovery, or if the medicine is wrong, a rapid surrender.

The Tullamore River joins the Clodiagh River below Rahan and in a little while the joint streams run into the Brosna. Somewhere before this last meeting we ran into a little Sargasso Sea. The whole surface of the river was so covered with weed that the water was practically invisible and we dragged ourselves along with the paddles with a great effort. This strenuous exercise continued for about a mile and when we joined the Brosna, I discovered, to our dismay, that all our spinners and line had disappeared from the stern where they had been lying to dry. It looked as if we would end this trip with only the tent left.

The Brosna is a very pretty river. The banks are well wooded and the country through which it flows is secluded and varied in scenery. We were told that it is a splendid fishing river and again I felt the foolishness of travelling without a rod. We passed Ferbane next day and as a blazing sun was now beating down upon us we drew ashore about a mile below the village and camped beside a little wood.

It transpired that we were to be blessed with a heat-wave, which was to last for ten days and the heat was so great that we put off further travelling from day to day until, before we knew it, the holidays were finished and this diminutive trip ended up as a sunbathing and swimming orgy.

We would rise at eight to find the camper's dream of a great blue sky and the long morning rays of the sun blazing across the trees. With such beneficence showing beneath 'the eyelids of the mórning' we started the day with a light heart. Joyous, if raucous, aubades sounded the welkin almost as soon as the birdsong and breakfast was prepared amidst a merry humming and whistling and snatches of lyrics,

Broom out the floor now, lay the fender by,
And plant this bee-sucked bough of woodbine there,
And let the window down...

We dined on enormous helpings of bacon, eggs and mushrooms, for in a field behind the wood we had discovered a larder of them. Benny maintained that there are about two hundred varieties of stools, and that about one hundred and ninety-nine of them are poisonous; but we had no ill effects and they were delicious.

After breakfast I went hunting with the bow and first morning out I bagged a sparrow-hawk in a tall pine tree. There were a great number of these hawks about and I suppose I was doing some farmer a favour by reducing the breed by one. Rabbits too, were plentiful.

As the day lengthened we would lie on the river bank, until we almost fried in the heat and then plunge into the river to cool. I remember that after a few days of this, when we were bathing several times a day, the sting of the water on our sun-baked skins caused us to yell out in agony; and we could stay scarcely longer than a minute in the water because of the pain. As we wore only bathing shorts the whole day through, we developed a remarkable tan that lasted the entire summer. In these idyllic surroundings we took to writing 'poetry', atrocious doggerel which we read and reviewed to each other amidst scathingly libellous criticisms. The aim was to outdo each other in banality and bathos.

There was a milkmaid who passed twice a day on the opposite bank. She was as plain-looking as a woman could be and we would banter her across the river, she replying in a stentorian voice, punctuated with peals of horse laughter. She, we made the heroine of a ballad, and daily added verses until it grew to a prodigious length, like the 'Cowboys' Lament'. We sang it to a number of catches, but as the verses were of varying metres and lengths we achieved no unity. We would serenade her as she passed, while she howled epithets at us, as we sat on the bank strumming imaginary guitars; and the wild strains of the 'Maid of Ferbane' disturbed the tranquil echoes of the woods.

Almost opposite our camp was a large field which a young farmer was engaged in ploughing throughout the heat of the day. He wore no shirt and we could see the remarkable contrast between the high colour of his neck and forearms and the lily-white texture of his torso. As farmers do not usually go in for sunbathing it looked as if this one was taking a leaf from our book. We lay on a hill above his field and watched him work. Anyone who has not so observed the industrious cannot say truthfully that they have tasted to the full the fruits of idleness. This feverish man plodded behind his steaming pair, now up the field, now down the field, now up again. It was a large field and there was a lot of ploughing in it. To look at him working was a delight and we would pass admiring words on his strength, his stamina, his pertinacity, and above all, his resigned bearing under the burning sun, until we could find no tributes further to praise this transcendental man. Occasionally we would wave to him an encouragement to keep up the good work and he, misinterpreting it, would wave resignedly back.

As we were singing rounds after tea one evening, a tall man came through a gap in the hedge above the tent and joined us. He asked did we do any shooting and I showed him the bow. This seemed to be the last thing he expected and he fondled it with wonder. We set off on a hunt with him and he brought us far afield to some deserted land that was plentiful with rabbits. Wandering back in the still summer evening he whispered that there would be good shooting the following evening, as he would bring us to a badger's earth. But he said, deprecatingly, 'Them ould arrows would bounce off a badger's hide like raindrops off a duck. But I'll bring you something to hold him.' And he smiled a secret smile.

Next evening he appeared again through the hedge and approached us slowly, with one hand behind his back. I was agog to see the deadly weapon he had brought, which I imagined to be an arrow with a game-head of razor sharpness, if not with a poisoned barb. 'Well, men, I think this'll bring ye a few badgers to hang outside yer tent.' And he produced a yard-long piece of solid steel with a well-ground point and notch for the string, but naturally with no flight. I looked at it in dismay.

'I'm afraid we'll never fire that, friend,' I said,

disappointment evident in my tone. 'Only a large crossbow would move that weapon any distance.' He thought I was joking, so I took the 'arrow', (which weighed about two pounds) and fitting it to the bow, drew a full string and fired. The 'arrow' dropped about two feet away with a dull heavy sound. I had to explain that lightness was the essential characteristic and that force was but the equation of lightness and speed, the flight giving direction. He was a sorely disappointed hunter for he had spent hours choosing, grinding and tempering his wonderful 'arrow'. I gave it back to him and told him to keep it; it might prove useful as a spear at close quarters. So we set off for the badger's den.

It was late in the evening when we arrived, picking our steps with the utmost caution and moving in silence. The earth was a short distance from the river, at the foot of a hill and was surrounded by trees. I took my post behind a bush about thirty yards from the burrows and Benny and our visitor moved away below them. I waited, crouching, for a long time, fingering my arrows and seeing that my sheath knife was loose and ready, just in case of necessity. I had on only canvas shoes and shorts and a light shirt, and was under no illusions about the power of a badger's jaws. Badger hunters are supposed to wear two pairs of trousers sewn together and filled between with cinders; for a badger, it is said, will not cease his bite until he hears the bone crunch.

I saw the first badger slowly poke his head out of a burrow and survey the land. Satisfied, he emerged, gave a low grunt and was followed by another. I watched uneasily as two more followed until there were four, probably a family, moving quietly about under the trees, their white-barred heads showing faintly in the last light. I had not bargained for such a brood, although it was a wonderful opportunity to test the bow.

I fitted the best arrow and aimed at the largest of the group, that was feeding at the bole of a chestnut. I drew back until the string passed my ear and could feel the strong pressure of the hemp through the leather fingerguard. Things happened quickly. The 'phutt' of the arrow was followed by a savage snarl and barks. The others ran back to the earth, but the victim had the arrow embedded in his back. He ran furiously around seeking his attacker. I instinctively rose to my feet and started to back up the hill, fitting another arrow as I did so. He saw me and growling in pain, commenced to scramble up the slope in pursuit. I fired again and missed, and as I hurriedly backed up the uneven ground, my foot slipped and I pitched on my side. The infuriated animal was very near, when there was a loud roar and our visitor appeared at a run. The badger stopped, saw the new danger and was apparently in doubt who to attack, when the two-pound 'arrow' landed within an inch of him. He turned and bolted back down the slope, disappearing down the burrow.

We picked up the remains of my arrow from the mouth of the den, where it had broken off when the animal had charged in. I was fully convinced of the old tales of the toughness of their hide and decided to give them a wide berth in the future, unless I had some proper game arrows and a pair of good strong boots.

The limit of our explorations was a trip or two downriver, principally to fish, for we had bought some more line and tackle at Ferbane. But we caught nothing. Kind-hearted fishers along the banks encouraged us with tales of fine fish caught in just such a pool, or by just such a bridge; but still we caught nothing. It may have been that we were using the wrong bait, or that the day was too sunny, or the river too low; but I took heart, for we one day spent a half-hour beside a taciturn fellow who fished with dry-fly, and that, they say, is a great intricate art. He waved his rod this way and that, he slowly coiled his long line in the air, drying the bait; he performed wizardries of wrist work that all but chucked his trout under the chin with the fly; yet, when we again passed him on the return journey, hours later, he had caught nothing. I am inclined to think that there is no play in the world like fishing – for learning patience.

The furthest run we made in our now crippled canoe was to the village of Belmont, about four miles from Shannon Harbour, which itself is about two miles from Banagher. The Grand Canal runs quite close to the Brosna here and joins the Shannon, with the Brosna, just beyond Shannon Harbour at Bullock Island. Those who would like to do a trip from Dublin to the Shannon could come by the Grand Canal to this point, and continue on to Portumna, only about ten miles south, where Lough Derg commences. The Shannon country around here is low-lying and flat, and not of great interest, but the big lake would well recompense travellers for the few uninteresting miles.

From a canoeist's point of view our trip was ridiculously short, but from the camper's it was of interest and very pleasant country in which to loiter. Incidentally, camp sites in Ireland are almost invariably free. I have never yet been asked to pay for a site and though I suppose it could happen, it is for all practicable purposes unheard of. Indeed, the good people will usually go to endless trouble to show you what they consider the ideal site; but this does not always correspond with the camper's ideal. Beware of camping in a field with cattle; they are the most curious of beasts and if a camper be unfortunate enough to leave his tent unattended, they will chew up everything in reach. In this respect they are as bad as goats. Also, no matter how tempting the spot in fair weather, keep away from trees: heavy raindrops from leaves will penetrate a tent easier than will the heaviest shower. Should the tent leak under heavy rain, throw a ground sheet over it to keep the blankets dry. And don't light the campfire within a foot or two of the tent, lest your roof for the night go up in flames from the sparks.

But you probably learned all this long ago with the boy scouts.

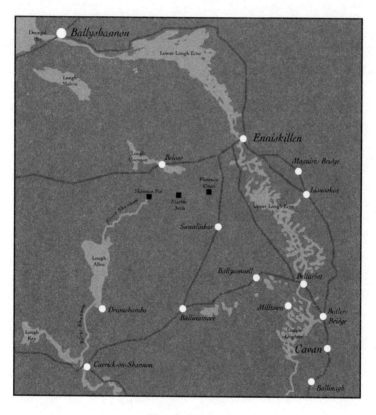

Lough Oughter

LOUGH OUGHTER

We took the train to Cavan town and without difficulty hired our usual gilly, again with donkey cart. Our gear was transported to the banks of the Cavan River, on which we had blithely hoped to start the cruise.

The Cavan River is a diminutive stream, so that when we had assembled the canoe and launched it, she looked enormous, rather like the Queen Mary on the Liffey, if I may use hyperbole for illustration. To add to our troubles, water immediately commenced to trickle along the bottom and, for a while, it looked as if the whole venture would end before ever it started. We waited anxiously, sitting on the bank and ruefully measuring with our eyes for almost an hour every drop that gathered. The specially strengthened sternpiece had been badly worn and holed, and I had stitched a doubled heavy canvas over this, using many coats of a flat oil paint to waterproof and stretch the canvas. Though at first this seemed a failure, it transpired later to be quite a reliable job and the leakage was very small, probably entering through some large stitching holes.

As the evening was lengthening and we always made first camp out of sight of town, we eventually decided to push off, fervently hoping our weight would not increase the leak. It did not. In a few minutes we were struggling with the youthful ebullience and manifold impediments of the Cavan River. It proved much too narrow for double-paddling; indeed, even with a single blade one had to go hunting for a clear spot to sweep. The stream was unfitted for anything except a duck or a floating can. It was about a foot deep, but was peppered with rocks, bends, shallows, broken bottles, snags, roots, trees – indeed, every conceivable obstruction. In about five minutes we gave up the hopeless task of paddling and put on our wading shoes. It took us all our time even to wade the river and to keep the canoe from being pitched into thorn trees or onto rocks.

There was much cursing, splashing, and falling about, and we did at least provide amusement for a lone herd or schoolboy, unused to seeing people walking down their river, towing a boat behind. Even when we came to deeper stretches there was a continual jumping into the river as we struck sudden shallows pocked with rusty tins, bicycles, and broken glassware of all descriptions. It was very late that evening when, after covering several miles, we came, thoroughly drenched, on the wide, quiet and comparatively deep stretch that heralded the beginning of canoeing proper. We camped beneath a well-timbered knoll, not a house in sight, and all about us the hush of summer. Later, we inspected *Minny* and were pleased to see that she had shipped very little water.

The early morning swim is a delightful thing – when it is over. The gooseflesh, the damp grass, the dank chilly air, the bleak prospect of the early river mist, all these have to be endured. The swim itself is pleasant enough, especially when the sun is shining, but the full zest of it is felt only when one has briskly towelled, run a mile or two, dressed and lazed almost on top of the camp-fire: the exhilarating smell of bacon, egg and beans mixed with wood-smoke whetting the appetite, if by this time any whetting be needed. How one eats at such a time.

🐚

We idled along the lazy waters and approached, with some trepidation, a little pond called Coalpit Lake: an ugly name enough. We had been warned in Cavan that every year there was a drowning in it. In fact, the year before we came two boys had capsized in a small boat and drowned. As often happened, while we were carefully watching and planning, we suddenly burst through a screen of reeds onto the little lake. What a commotion we caused!

It was a tiny place, little bigger than a park pond, a sort of flooded morass or bog. On the left hand or north side, a thick belt of trees fringed the gloomy pond, while a wide circle of reeds swept around the rest of its perimeter. Sticks and dead trees stuck out at its black bottom at all angles. But what struck us most was the immense congregation of wild duck. Every duck in Co Cavan seemed to have come to this secluded place to nest, for they shot backwards and forwards over the water, quacking and shepherding young into the reeds. The hens spattered all over the lake, many playing the 'broken wing' trick to lure us from the young, which jerked in schools into the nearest reeds. In a matter of minutes there was not a duck to be seen, though the reeds must have been thick with them.

They had a secure nesting, as I had to stand in the prow and direct Benny to paddle with extreme care to clear the snags, many of which rested just under water and were visible only from a standing position. We were very glad to clear the place, as it certainly could be a death trap, more especially on a windy day.

The Cavan River, now in adolescence, flowed on by Farnham woods, through which we rambled to stretch our legs, finding the freshly killed body of a red squirrel with talon marks on the belly. We passed through silent little Swan Lake and shortly emerged onto the broader waters of the Annalee River, tumbling boisterously towards Lough Oughter. Here we caught a few perch, which were a welcome addition to table at the next meal.

Our leak seemed to have closed up completely, no bilge now being found in our bottom in the evening. We bought our food supply for lake travel at Butlersbridge and here unearthed in the ancient post office a store of quaint, antiquated postcards, which we despatched to friends. Heaven only knows how long these brilliantly coloured cards had lain in their dusty boxes awaiting the rare visitor to Butlersbridge. Flamboyant sunsets, exotic birds falling to the gun and demure overdressed women peeping from under gaudy parasols greeted the half-awakened eyes of friends and relations, who may have thought that they had been whisked by some weird time-machine to the more leisured days of a quieter century.

In the evening we hailed the first of the Oughter lake chain, Carratraw, in the teeth of a strong wind that set the shallow waters boiling into foam. It would have been a difficult matter to have sought one's way out of this lake without compass or map, for armlets disappeared in every direction, and as can be seen from the map, Lough Oughter is a jigsaw puzzle of lakes lying cheek by jowl, the wear of time and weather gradually knitting them together by shallow channels. Those waters are safe for canoeing, the landbreaks are never far apart and the lakes are, to a great extent, shallow. Little evidence of life was to be seen, except for a distant smoke spiral or glimpse of gable among the woods that marched by the shores.

Very early in the morning I was astir with the rifle. The day broke cold and bleak, a steady wind rattling the branches of the oaks about the tent. The half-light fell on the metallic surface of the lake, throwing the islands into shadowy relief and etching with a colourless monotony the open waters. I caught sight of a coot dipping among the twittering reeds and shot him, having to take out the canoe to fetch him. I had never eaten coot, nor did I know if they were edible, but this was a fine plump bird, and I put him by for dinner. On higher ground I added a hare to the foodstore and satisfied with the morning's takings, rambled back to camp; Benny, like a good scout, having the breakfast cooked. There is nothing so pleasing to the early riser as finding the camp alive, the fire glowing and the victuals ready, after a prowl through the cold damp air and grasses in the dawn. One fears for the salvation of the sluggard soul who is found snoring, having even filched his mate's blankets in the interval. Leave him, for the future, in his city.

The cooking of the coot was attended with much ceremony on my part, taking my job of cook seriously and with much banter from my companion. He declared he had no intention of risking his precious gastric juices on such dubious fare. I rigged a spit over the fire, as to the manner born, and having plucked, drawn, and trussed the bird, I sat patiently basting it with butter and its own juice; a tiresome proceeding, as the capricious wind flung the acrid smoke of the fire in my eyes no matter where I squatted. When all the rest of the dinner, beans, potatoes, even tea, was ready, still I sat patiently basting, my eyes red and running water from the smoke, and the old coot or 'old boot' as Benny impiously termed it, seeming merely to get tougher and tougher. The fork fairly whanged off it when I attempted to probe it for tenderness and I feared that there was some esoteric rite, some dark secret of the kitchen, which I knew not, essential to its cooking. I believe I could be there yet, patiently basting and blunting the fork on it but that hunger would not wait longer. We took it down. Attempting to cut it proved a joke, the knife merely running back and forth as on a motor tyre. We eventually tore it to pieces and found it wholesome and succulent but of an indescribable toughness. The teeth hardly penetrated it and our jaws tired from chewing. Though we kept some for a cold supper and again exercised our jaw muscles, even the most enthusiastic optimist would not call it a success. I think now we ate it too fresh and should have let it hang in the manner of game. We shot no more, but some camper, better schooled in culinary mysteries, can be assured that it looks a promising bird and worth experiment.

We zig-zagged out of Carratraw into Lough Ougher proper, making our way by compass and map in the general direction of Killeshandra, that we might not be too far from a victualling centre, for these lakes are very isolated. The lakes are a maze and the channels very shallow. I can imagine that, in a dry spell, many of these channels would be dry and the canoeist would have to make portage.

We visited Cloughoughter Castle on Inch Island, a gaunt weird ruin, occupying its tiny islet to the lake edge. It was a solid structure in its day, this O'Reilly fortress, and the local people say that there is an underground passage leading from the castle to the mainland. Owen Roe O'Neill died here in 1649 having, it is said, been poisoned by an English agent. Remember Davis' line, 'And he died at Cloch Uachtar, upon St Leonard's Day'?

We camped on Eonish Island at the southern end of the lake. Here, at the eastern extremity of the island, the lake opened out to north and south, while in the centre of the channel a small island acted as a windbreak. Woods spread along the contiguous shores and the spot was sheltered and peaceful. Behind us, beyond a grove of trees, was a series of small meadows, broken by bracken and copses, while the southern shore was strewn with boulders. Above these were the remains of a homestead, the boundaries of the gardens extant, the earth covered with a lush short grass. A ruined orchard, surrounded by thorn trees, extended up to the fields. The island abounded in rabbits.

We spent a week in this delightful spot, making friends with the young farmer whose family was the sole occupant of this fairly extensive island. The man had a flat-bottomed boat which he had built himself, as many of the littoral residents of the midland lakes do. To us, she seemed to leak like a sieve, but this does not concern these hardy boatmen, who spend as much time baling as rowing. We went boating in the evenings with him and shooting rabbits in the old orchard, his double-barrelled shotgun bowling them over three to our one. The rabbits were mostly young and very tender. We boiled them first, afterwards frying them in butter with bacon and though I am not partial to shop rabbits, here in the open country, these graziers, freshly killed, were delicious.

The weather was dry and sunny, the wind dropping on the second day leaving the field to the sun. We fished for perch and caught many, the lake apparently teeming with them. Swimming became a daily habit again, for strangely enough, when spending all your time on water the urge seems to leave you, except on very hot days; whereas in the city you will barge out anytime for a plunge.

A wonderfully restful feeling comes over me near water. Especially so when camped out amongst rivers and lakes. Merely to sit and stare out over the still waters brings a flood of contentment to the soul, while to glide over them in a canoe or a small boat is as near to absolute peace as can be found. Have you ever noticed how people will lean over the side of a boat staring into the water and lovingly trail the hand through it, as though in caress? There is some deeper meaning here, if we but knew it, akin to the urge that drives crowds to the sea, even to overcrowded beaches, to spas, to lakes, as if a thirst for the solace that only water can give. Perhaps baptism is the highest symbolism of this mystery, 'Unless you be born again of water', signifying purification and the return of lost innocence. Indeed, if the earth be four-fifths water, out of what deep and fabulous mystery was this conceived?

There was another soul who likewise found his peace on water, and, indeed, he seemed to go ashore only to sleep. This persistent fisher was abroad at all hours of the day and night and, in his time, must have murdered whole hecatombs of perch. We labelled him 'Dangerous Dan' for his dogged purpose. Even on downright wet days or in the strongest wind his little punt could be seen lying alongside the bank or bobbing over the open lake, heavy laden with perch. It seemed he had a private war against the fish of Lough Oughter, a veritable *cacoethes piscandi*. He was, I believe, an Englishman who, happening on the quiet town of Killeshandra, lost his heart to the peace of the place and its splendid background of lakes, sold out and settled there, where he opened a small shop. Certainly he was catching up on the lost hours he may have spent in a dusty office or factory at some industrial city. How I envied him. He made his own spinners and bait, several specimens of which were on view in the shop. But the shop was closed whenever we passed; there was more important business afoot.

The runs to Killeshandra were very pleasant. A delightful little shooting lodge at Killykeen, standing on a vivid green terrace of lawn among the woods, marked the channel connecting Upper and Lower Lough Oughter. Duck, coot and waterfowl were plentiful, providing difficult targets in the distant reeds. From Oughter one passes through Tullyguide and Town lakes and a river into Killeshandra, which tumbles from its hills right down to the lake shore, providing a most picturesque scene from the lake. The people of Killeshandra we found extremely friendly and helpful, the food reasonable, the meals well cooked and copious. We took a great liking to it and made friends even on our short visits. It was understandable why the Englishman had chosen to take his leisure here.

Filled one day with the good cheer of Killeshandra and our food bag spilling its overflowing viands like a cornucopia onto the bottom of the canoe, we bustled along the little river leading from Town lake to Oughter.   We were singing 'Fortissimo con fuoco', some stirring ballad of plunder and martial glory, and throwing our wonted caution to the winds, when there was a long scraping sound and the canoe suddenly rose high in the water and came to a sudden stop. Simultaneously a sizeable gush of water poured downward from the prow. We were flabbergasted but stayed quite still, the song, as it were, suspended above our heads, waiting for our beloved *Minny* to sink slowly with a sad gurgle to her untimely end. Nothing happened, so we cautiously poled against the shallow bottom with the paddles, and, again to the accompaniment of that horrible scraping noise, she slowly backed off the obstacle, and to our joy, showed no sign at sinking. The water had been bilge lying in the prow, but had looked uncommonly like a spout from a big leak. We had driven full tilt onto a concealed stake which, in low water, would have been visible. The river had many of these dangerous obstacles, seemingly there to stretch wire across the stream, though what the object was we could not fathom. They were useless as cattle barriers, for in high water a beast could be trapped on them. They are a great danger to a canoeist, a wary eye and a quick wrist being essential to avoid them. Bottom inspection showed a long weal on our craft, but nothing more serious than scraping of the paint. The fabric of these canoes is indeed tough, though of course this sort of careless paddling does not improve matters.

Arrival at camp heralded further disaster. Across the lake we sighted cattle browsing by the tent and we put on speed, though too late. The herd, all young bullocks, had commenced depredations, though no doubt we had arrived in time to prevent further damage. We found that a towel and a pound of butter had been eaten. Plates and mugs were trodden on and badly buckled, several guys and the tent door badly chewed, and books ripped. Of all the enemies of campers, cattle are by far the worst. No matter how innocent they look, or how far away they graze, or what apparently impenetrable barriers seem to fence them safely from you – still they will find a way to satisfy their insatiable curiosity. It is never safe to leave a cup unattended for long once the tell-tale turd, no matter how old, is discovered. They will spring up out of the ground at you, or drop from the skies, but be sure that the ubiquitous nuisances will be there to chew your food and your tent to pieces once you turn your back.

I liked the evenings best. Long midsummer twilights fell over the lake and the islands, quieting the wind and the little waves, hushing the twittering of leaves, and limning the silent shore in soft golds and bronzes. At such a time a voice carried far over the still waters, the lonely call of a curlew or the distant cooing of pigeon came with startling clearness, out of the empty silence. Stalking noiselessly through the dewing grasses after small game, the full thrill of the hunt filled one with a sharp alertness; the ears pricked for the breaking of a twig or rustle of a leaf and the eye caught the subtle hint of shade amongst the undergrowth or bracken that warned of the quarry. Such tracking brings out the instinct of the hunter, latent in man, and the deadly earnestness of the chase that comes whether the game be big or small heightens the senses to a knifelike sharpness. At such a time the veneer of conventional living slips off like a cloak and one is part of the wild life of the woods and rivers, glorying in the beauty of the setting, and exulting in the lordship of man. Only when the night falls and the stars are out, when the trees are a shapeless bulk, and the lake a dark silent pool, does one feel the call of the firelight; and returns to the tenuous protection of the tent - for at heart we are gregarious.

Some friends came by motorcycle from Dublin to visit us for the day. There was much ferrying across an arm of the lake to bring them to Eonish. We spent the evening target shooting. Ferrying back was arduous owing to a strong wind that whipped up sharp little waves and made landing difficult. We lost our way in a plantation seeking a shortcut to Killeshandra and, indeed, it must be a rare thing to do. For there is no doubt that this country is greatly tree-starved. Out of about seventeen million acres in the twenty-six counties only one quarter of a million acres, or less than 1.5% are wooded. Everywhere we went we sought for woods, but always they were diminutive places. Indeed, one could walk through most of our 'woods' in fifteen minutes. As a lover of nature I deplored this poverty, but from a purely practical point of view, though I know nothing of the subject, I believe that woods are a great advantage to a country. Certainly they provide shelter and windbreaks and too, no doubt, on mountainous country would act as soil conservors, not to speak of their role in industry. Our Forestry Department is supposed to be endeavouring to overcome this great national scarcity but, in various travels around Ireland, the attempts to re-tree the country seem pitifully inadequate.

In these days of enormous urban development, we seem, alas, to have forgotten completely to provide wide open spaces to which the walled-in dwellers, in the few days they have in the year, might go to open their lungs (and their minds) to find a little peace and quiet in the midst of natural beauties. The effect of such healthy and clean play on the youth of the country would not only be reflected in the physical sphere but would, in a more important one, go far towards freeing the mind from the all too insistent fripperies and wasteful trifles of the times. The aim could not be better headlined than in the old Greek motto *Mens sana in corpore sano*.

At present one has to risk trespassing if a few days are to be spent in the open country; or permission sought from some landowner for fishing or shooting rights – often grudgingly given or charged for exorbitantly. There seems to be no provision made for the man of small means who wishes to indulge in the harmless and healthy outdoor pleasures that have been almost everywhere abrogated by the wealthy.

This trip, therefore, again resolved itself into a short canoe run, a good camping spot in pleasant surroundings and lots of loafing, sunbathing, reading, swimming, and messing about in the canoe on short fishing or exploration trips. Then, another short run to the railhead for home: infinitely to be preferred to a slavish timetable schedule allowing of so many hours or days for this spot and that, and seeing things because it is felt that they should be seen, irrespective of whether one is interested or not in seeing them. We lazed back through pleasant mazes of peninsulas and islands, potting at duck and plover and snipe on the way. We came to the Erne, a stately river, flowing richly through fat meadows and undulating land, crammed, I believe, with salmon and trout. Rises were numerous. And of course we had no rod. Consequently, rises were sure to be numerous.

One evening, as we were dozing in the tent after a meal, we were startled by the loud blast of a shotgun, followed by a rain of pellets on the fabric. We rushed out and beheld a pair of lunatics firing at a flock of terns which were dipping and wheeling over the broad river. We harangued them roundly for their foolishness, for, in addition to the danger of the canoe being punctured, we ourselves could have been injured by the stray shot. We found, later, a wounded tern helplessly swimming about on the river. I brought it ashore and endeavoured to mend a wing which had been bruised by a pellet. Not, I fear, with much success, for when we let it free it continued making pitiful efforts to fly; though maybe in time the wing may have healed.

We passed through Carrifin Lake, a singularly quiet little sheet of water, and on again to the Erne, now broadening and deepening as it progressed. As the river approaches Belturbet it breaks into shallows abounding in rocks. Here we drew ashore and after having a fairly long abstemious spell, we took our delight in pints of ale, always rendered more precious when drunk in the morning or afternoon, knowing that everyone is about their business.

Thus Oughter. It is to be recommended for its peace, its quietness, its little woods, its hopelessly muddled byways and inlets and its lack of things that one must see. There is nothing 'to see', consequently guidebooks ignore it. Go there if you want to get away from cities and towns, and desire to laze among fish and fowl, uninterrupted even by peasants. They, too, are rare enough and when met, pleasant peasants.

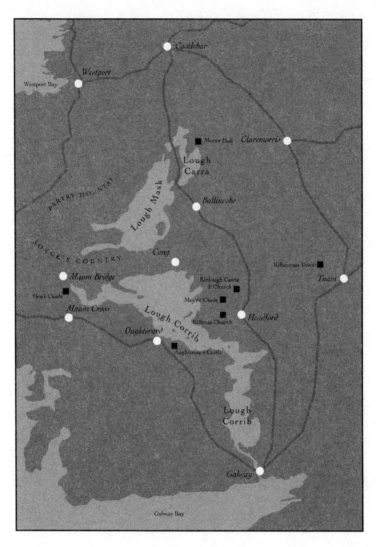

The Corrib Lakes

THE CORRIB LAKES

These are big lakes and should be treated with respect by canoeists. Also, they are treacherous lakes and to be treated with great wariness and circumspection. Galway, of course, is the ideal starting point, though a trip could be commenced at Cong and done southwards.

We found a convenient spot to assemble the canoe beside the boathouse of the Galway Rowing Club; a smooth green on the Corrib River. But it was dropping a fine rain and the visibility was nil when we built *Minny* and pushed a mile or two upriver to seek our first camping spot. This time there were three of us and we planned that one should walk and meet the canoeists at previously agreed meeting places, changing hands at each spot. It was an experiment and not a very successful one.

Sunday morning came with a weak sun and a strong wind. Ferrying to the far bank to walk to Mass, one of the party pitched into the river and had to be carried back to the camp to change clothes. This was an inauspicious start. Neither of my companions had ever before been in a canoe and I felt nervous and responsible about bringing them up to these big lakes in a canoe now nearly eight years old.

We found a clean public house-cum-grocery-cum-hotel and agreed, in the event of our becoming separated, to meet at this place. This foresight was later rewarded. We also bought a stock of spinners and fishing line, and a large provision load.

Back at camp we planned the first journey. Dick was to walk

from Menlough to Clooniff headland, a little promontory at the southern end of the lake, just beyond where the lake flows into the Corrib River. We worked out the mileage by road and water, and expected to meet about six o'clock. So Dick took to the road, while Mick and I pushed upriver, loaded with equipment for three, which left the canoe very low in the water.

The river was down, it being high summer and I noted how rocky the bottom was. These were sharp limestone rocks, pitted with holes that had a razor-like edge, so that one had to be extra careful in avoiding bumps and groundings which would be of little consequence in rivers with rounded or weed-covered stones. Mick took easily to canoeing and once out of the shallows began to pick up the rhythm of paddling. Soon the river broadened and I sensed the feel of lake water. We were discussing how our arrangements would work out, Mick being very dubious about it. I, on the contrary, was optimistic, feeling it incumbent on me to give the air of everything going well. But indeed I was surprised at the exactness of the calculations when, as we turned the bend of the island that led us out onto the lake, Dick walked over the hill behind Clooniff and reached the shore almost at the same time as ourselves. It was fortuitous, of course, the thing was too perfect. But as I greeted him, 'Mr M......, I presume?,' I expanded on the fool-proofness of the idea and soon had them convinced. I wish I had been.

We camped by the shore, near a thicket of thorn trees that held off a strong wind which seemed to blow unceasingly. The farmer, upon whose land we were camped, came around and shared a mug of tea and cheese sandwiches with us. He warned us that the Corrib was a dangerous lake, full of rocks and unexpected shallows, and advised us to follow the channel markers. These markers, large towers painted white and black, had been erected to guide the steamers of the Corrib Steam Navigation Co which traded here half a century ago.

Early, before the dawn, I rose and took the gun. The light was poor and the outcrop of great limestone rocks that strewed the lake edge were barely visible. So that I felt I had done a good morning's work when I shot a snipe perched on a distant rock, the bird being visible only through its slight movements. Alas, for the pride of the hunter. When I fetched it the bird turned out to be a tiny thing, hardly bigger than a sparrow, of what species I know not. But a howl of derision greeted me when I brought it back to camp.

We spent the day hunting for wild duck on the far shore. Although we saw them disappearing into the reeds upon our approach and though we remained anchored deep in the reeds for an hour without making a sound; still, the wily birds were not to be caught out so easily. Not a solitary, foolhardy bill was shown. For alertness and cautiousness it takes a rare bird to beat the duck.

The lake at this southern end was extremely shallow. Sharp, dangerous rocks, sometimes but inches under the surface, stretched everywhere. As the day was calm I sat up on the stern backrest when patrolling and thus we could pick a safe passage through them. In the afternoon, the wind rose and again blew strongly, whipping up long, white-capped rollers. We decided to stay another night here in the hope of a calm. But it blew all night and the next morning without decreasing.

One gets bored sitting looking over lakes waiting on them to assume that mirror-like surface with which most of us picture them. Though by the afternoon the wind had strengthened, we decided to risk the lake and to push on towards the northern shores. We again picked our meeting place, this time at the romantic-sounding inlet of Currawatia, where we estimated to meet at six o'clock. Dick again volunteered to do the hiking. Mick and I fixed the spraysheets tightly on the combings and with a last anxious look at the wide stretch of angry whitecaps that filled the lake, we pushed out before the wind. I can imagine how my companion felt on experiencing his first taste of rough water.

The lake was in a dirty mood. The sun shone brightly, but the wind blew with a considerable force, lashing the waters into a broken fury. We had gone only a few yards when I feared for the canoe and advised my companion to turn back towards land. We made this attempt, but gave it up immediately, for, as soon as we tried to turn, the wind and waves caught us broadside and well-nigh capsized us. Our minds thus made up for us, we plunged out to the centre of the lake and I knew we would not be at Currawatia at six o'clock. We gave up all ideas of making for the white marker, our whole attention being devoted to keeping our head on to the waves and our stern to the wind. We headed for the land nearest to this forced direction and this meant that we had to cross the lake at a long diagonal that took us across its greatest width.

I had experienced this weather before, but then the canoe was tolerably new and carried equipment for two only. Now she was old and patched and in addition to carrying gear for three, the sudden shallows of the Corrib were an added danger. It was no weather for her. As I felt her heave and slough back in the big troughs, all her light joints creaking in protest, and her sixteenth-of-an-inch canvas flapping against the flooring, I wondered if she would ever make it. I vowed to give her honourable retirement in a mill pond if she should. Indeed, I never so appreciated Panurge's pitiful blubberings and his soulful cry, 'O twice and thrice happy those who stay at home and plant cabbages.'

In the middle of the lake we could see how far off our course we were. Instead of heading northwest, we had been driven northeast. The waves were really big here, yet sometimes, after having been pitched and rolled and drenched all over, we would enter a stretch of comparative calm. It was then an odd thing to move evenly through and to see large rollers pass by but a few yards away while we seemed to saunter between them in an enchanted boat.

We drove rapidly in towards land after an anxious passage and could see the usual Corrib coast – ugly honeycombed rocks ringing the coarse grass and the thick belt of hazels. I jumped out up to the waist in the water to slow our pace and eased her through the stones. Looking at my watch I saw that we had crossed a good four miles of lake under forty-five minutes. We had paddled only to keep our way or top a wave – the wind had brought us over. I could imagine what a pace a sailingboat would have made in that wind, but there was not a boat of any description to be seen on the lake.

We thought we had landed on an island and made our way inland coming on a secluded hamlet of thatched cottages surrounded by tall trees. We enquired our whereabouts of an aged peasant, clad in the famous bawneen coat and discovered that we were on the mainland, in a place called Annaghdown, where there was neither shop nor telephone. We were directed to the townland at Coolbwe, to 'Raygan's Pub' for groceries. This was a weary walk of several miles, but we replenished our depleted victuals and solaced ourselves with ale. Coming back, we borrowed a lift in a car to the garda barracks of Corundulla and had a message put through to Moycullen on the far shore of the lake, asking the gardaí there to get word to Tullowkyne where Dick was to await us if we missed him at the foreshore at Currawatia. This, we thought, would at least put his mind at ease about us.

We took a shorter road back to the lake, but still we had done about eleven miles walking when we arrived, in the pitch darkness of midnight, not having eaten since breakfast at 10 a.m. The tent was pitched by torchlight and at 1 a.m. we set about making dinner – an unearthly hour. And all the time the strong wind blew, and the murmur of the troubled lake was audible all around.

It was a most persistent wind. Even in the grey, empty hour before dawn, when one is almost entitled to expect a lull, it blew without a pause, keeping the white horses at a brisk canter and shaking the long grasses from their roots. Heavy showers came down at intervals, then quickly ceased, the sun following immediately, but without warmth. We sat patiently on the foreshore, gazing anxiously over the lake to Tullowkyne Castle, which looked so near. At 6 p.m. we had had enough at it and, sink or swim, we clamped on the spraysheets and battered our way in rain and spray towards our tantalising landmark. We walked into the public house at Tullowkyne at 7 p.m. – twenty-five hours behind schedule. The best-laid plans had gone agley.

Dick had been there the previous night at 6 p.m. He was on time. He had waited until 10 p.m. and then, there being no place to sleep in Tullowkyne (also not foreseen) had walked back to the farmer's house at Clooniffe. There, as he later told us, he was kindly put to bed on the settle in the kitchen. In the morning he had walked back to Tullowkyne, waited patiently all day and there being no sign of us he had walked back to Galway, altogether walking twenty-eight miles that day. In Galway he had notified the gardaí and ordered a motor launch for the next day to search the lake. He was convinced that we had gone down. Nor had the gardaí in Moycullen transmitted our message to him; this little job, had it been done, would have saved him endless anxiety and fatigue. Indeed, when we met him that night in the agreed place, after we had borrowed lifts in three different cars to Galway, he looked worn out and was too worried even to grin at our unexpected re-appearance.

We took it easy for a few days on the shore at Currawatia. It is a desolate place, as is most of the shore of the southern lake. Only an isolated house or group of thatched dwellings were scattered at rare intervals along the coast. We spent the days shooting rabbits or hunting wild duck, this latter proving of absorbing interest, for shooting duck with a rifle is eighty per cent stalking, ten per cent sure shooting, and ten per cent luck. The stalking is the thing. Crawling over rocks or puddles on your belly, hiding the face and hands, pausing for an infinitely careful glance to see that the quarry is still there, finding the last safe shelter, and the agonisingly slow positioning of the gun; these constitute the real thrill of the hunt. But one nearly always comes back without the duck. These birds are uncanny, the way they sense humans. If you really want a duck and are not prepared for the savour of the chase, bring a shotgun. Or buy one at the poulterers when next in town.

The nights were moonless but bright with stars. With a great log fire crackling merrily, it was considered a delicacy of camp fare to burn black in the embers sweet new potatoes and to eat them running with melted butter. Lying on my back before the fire, in a dreamy crapulous contentment, the swish of waters, as it were, flowing through my idle mind, I picked out the summer constellations, Cassiopeia, Andromeda, the Dragon, Pegasus and, like a ribbon of mist binding the freckled brow of the night, the incalculable legions of the Milky Way. I could gaze for hours into the hosts, the words of the psalmist coming unbidden, 'The fool hath said in his heart, there is no God.' There is no finer way of calming the soul and no better conditioning for a quiet sleep, than reflection under the open sky and an easy conscience.

We changed the 'crew' for the next run. Mick took to the road, Dick and I setting out in, for once, calm weather. It was sunny, with occasional light showers and we took it easy, following the well-marked channel towards the narrows where the upper and lower lakes join. It was easy to see why the lakes had a bad name for boating. Occasionally poking among islands we would leave the channel and quite often glide over a gigantic rock but a bare few inches below the surface. In choppy water these treacherous rocks would not be visible and a boat, especially a sailing boat, would be driven onto their jagged surface before anything could be done about it. The extraordinary part of it was that the rocks were seen even in otherwise deep water, where they would never be expected. This is different from most Irish lakes where, when one is in deep water, it can reasonably be expected to be free of obstacles.

Approaching Ferry Point, where the lakes join, I became uncomfortably aware of a great amount of bilge which reached over the floor level near the stern, so that I was sitting well in it. I said nothing to Dick, not willing to alarm him. As he sat in the forward end, it was not noticed by him, for, our greatest weight being in the stern, all bilge water collected there. It was comforting to reach the meeting place and to meet Mick without mishap. When we spilled out the canoe I was astonished at the amount of water we had shipped, but the others, knowing nothing of canoes, took no heed of it. Nevertheless, I thought hard on a plan to avoid the long run up the upper lake, the larger and more open of the two, for I could see that the old canoe was not fit to take a further punishing. We camped for the night facing the upper lake, which looked a great size and not a bit attractive, as the wind was up again stirring the white-cape to the furthest shores.

It was while walking to Mass the next day, passing a horse-cart on the white lime-dusted road, that I solved the problem of the upper lake. It was born more of discretion than of courage, and I fought hard with my conscience to settle for discretion, conscience gibing with a meaner word, thus:

I: 'Of course, when faced with obvious failure, it behoves one to consider all other means of attaining the goal. Now discretion, they say, is the better part of valour...'

Conscience: 'Who, pray, are "they", whom you so glibly quote?'

I: 'You are a very ignorant person, or ill read, not to know that proverbs are the philosophy of the generations, a condensed wisdom which any man may carry around in his head against the wiles of the Fates, without wasting years of his life studying a lot of drivel euphemistically termed philosophy, and about which men may argue or come to blows, without ever making head or tail of it. Take the Germans...'

Conscience: 'It you have no regard for philosophy, why do you truck with the sweepings and gew-gaws of that noble science? Everyone knows that these snippets of pocket-wisdom are a fraud and any cheap slogan can be immediately contradicted by another and a cheaper one. As, for instance, when a person says, "A rolling stone gathers no moss", his friend can confound him by replying, "A moored ship fills no holds."'

I: 'I don't recall hearing that last one, but you have a point there.'

Conscience: 'There you are, you see, you accept it, while I made it up to show you that any foolishness can be quoted as wisdom, when there is no authority to be named. Now for discretion...'

But I shut him up in his box and before I could change my mind I walked into the first public house I could find and blurted out to the man-of-the-house that we wanted transport to Oughterard for ourselves and bags. Oughterard was about seventeen miles away. He studied us closely far a while and answered 'Two quid,' without blushing.

'That's a fabulous price,' I replied, 'We could get to Dublin for that. Surely to God there's a cheaper way of getting to Oughterard in a horse and cart than by paying a ransom. Now, say five shillings.' At which he roared laughing. 'I thought ye were English,' he said, 'And ye from Dublin? Well, now...'

So we got down to bargaining and, after many drinks, which, in the Irish way, cost us as much again, we settled for the figure of ten shillings. I do not mean to imply that this honest peasant had a special price for unfortunate Englishmen only. He tried it on us, too, but when he saw that we had little money he did it cheerfully for the lesser figure. If you had come from the Blaskets and looked prosperous, (if that were possible) he would charge you £2 if you were fool enough to pay. It is a way they have in Inishmuck, where money is dear.

Incidentally, in this little spot on the fringe of Connemara, I met the world's champion knitter. For I enquired for two pairs of bawneen socks, those rugged, toastwarm, hand-knitted woollens that are famous for comfort and long wear; and being recommended to an old blind woman, I left my order. Lo and behold, the following day, as we all piled into the cart with our multitudinous baggage, an urchin came running down and handed me the damp, newly-knitted socks. I was told she had knitted them since yester evening. I wonder? Maybe she was in league with the Shee.

The road from Inishmuck to Oughterard is a white road, a dusty road, a knobbly road, a road bordered by rock-strewn hills and little fields. In parts we had to clamber out and push the cart. But the pony was lazy, his belly bursting with the easy grass of summer, so that he would not be extended. We passed strange hills strewn with grotesque rocks, small fields ploughed with endless trouble among the stones and little copses from which the crimson-berried mountain ash blazed like a flame. We passed a group of tinkers camped beside the roadside – the man bearded and bronzed, the woman, slatternly and dishevelled, tending the fire, their little, ragged bivouac a thing of myriad patches; and their wares were strewn in confusion around the grass.

At Oughterard we settled with our carrier and built again the canoe. We set out in calm water, for we were here in the lee of the wind, to make for a small island about half-a-mile away. But the island proved to be bleak and shelterless and it came on to rain, so that we returned to the foreshore to set up camp. All the foreshore was bogland and after much searching we found a patch dry enough to hold the tent, being surrounded by pools. Then the rain grew heavier and became a continuous downpour that lasted all the night and the next day, until we awoke to find ourselves islanded by water, so that if the groundsheet were lifted the earth below was found to be sodden.

Minny's days were nearly over. For, on the second day, when the weather cleared, we took her out to travel to Inchagill, the largest and most inviting of the many islands with which the upper lake is filled; but on putting out she filled rapidly and we returned in haste, in time only to jump into the shallows before she sank. Inspection showed a hole about two inches long beneath the sternpiece, where the fabric had worn through. She was beyond a quick repair, so that we were obliged, in sorrow, to pack her and spend the last few days 'marooned' on the mainland. She was a gallant little craft, and had done her share nobly, for these few trips which I have mentioned were only a small part of her journeys. She had been handled not too gently in her comparatively long life and had stood up stoutly to rough usage of many kinds. From her I learned a great respect and love for collapsibles, so that I resolved to replace her with another as soon as was practicable, to explore the very many fine waterways which still remained to us.

And, with solicitude, she laid us gently in a foot of water at the end. It could have been worse.